AF264508

the juice is worth the squeeze

a guide for swim coaches on managing a sucessful team

aaron dorfman

dedicated to my dearest corinne...

"she's as sweet, as tupelo honey,

she's an angel of the first degree,

she's as sweet as tupelo honey,

just like honey, baby, from the bee."

-van morrison

Introduction

I'm a firm believer that true love and art genuinely comes from the heart. *The Juice is Worth the Squeeze* is a passion project of mine and I'm proud I finished it. Everything in this book came straight from my heart.

Several people read the manuscript before I went to editing and the reviews were mixed. A few people questioned the title of the book. What does it mean? How does it relate to swimming and coaches?

My grandmother loved lemon water. She thought it cured everything. The flu. A headache. Anything. One day, we were standing in the kitchen and she cut a lemon in half. I was handed one of the halves. Grandma Rose wanted me to make a pitcher of lemon water for the afternoon and then another for the remainder of the week. Now, I didn't think the stuff was amazing but according to her, it was the panacea. I twisted and squeezed the fruit for a couple minutes. A few drops of juice out oozed out so I turned to her with anguish. She nodded, smiled and then said, "Keep working on it." I squeezed harder and finally, more came out. I mixed the water with a wooden spoon.

I tasted the lemon water and it was better than I thought. In fact, I enjoyed it! The stronger flavor came from my relentless effort to get more juice out of the fruit. And then, she said it. "The Juice is Worth the Squeeze." If I quit when I wanted to, I'd have weak flavored water.

The title of the book doesn't sound relatable to swim coaches. Once you get into it, you'll see how this mindset captures the essence of coaching. Moreover, the content provides drivers and guideposts to help you improve your deliverables and outcomes. Use this is a resource to help you launch an amazing and sustainable career in coaching.

I feel good about the work I've put into this project. I hope you enjoy it as much as I did writing it.

Meet Lineup

Chapter 1: Do What You Love

Do what you love and love what you do. Do what you love and the money will come. Do what you love and you'll never work a day in your life. Life is all about following your heart and passion.

How many times have you heard these clichés about making a career choice? Plenty, I'm sure.

When people asked why I selected swim coaching as a profession, I chose to respond with canned answers. I'd say I enjoyed helping children reach their full potential or that coaching came naturally to me. But really, I had one defining moment that solidified my desire to coach.

Do you know what raw emotion is? I never knew what it was before my first experience working with children. At seventeen, I volunteered as a coach at a local YMCA swim team. By my teenage standards, a volunteer job had to be fun, easy, and no more than five minutes from my house.

I supported an assistant coach with the younger groups. Essentially, I worked with recent swim class graduates in the new pre-competitive program. Swim team was their first shot in the "big show."

One day, as two dozen 14-and-younger children paraded out to the pool for practice, a couple girls lagged behind. The head coach guided the group to the large six-lane outdoor pool on this 65-degree morning. With steam rising from the pool, I held the hands of two stragglers and guided them to the lawn chairs next to the dive well.

"I'm scared to swim across the big pool," the younger girl said, anxious and shivering with her towel wrapped around her.

"There's nothing to be afraid of. It's nearly the same length as the indoor pool. You'll be fine," I said while she nodded in agreement.

The other child watched the athletes, now warming up, swimming butterfly. "I only know how to swim two strokes," she said. "I don't know how to do the one with two arms."

"The reason we're here is to help and support you. It's a short season, but you can learn all the strokes and improve. The first step is getting in the water," I said.

I worked with those two girls for much of that season. The older girl, Nelly, swam illegal butterfly all summer. She wanted to enter butterfly at the championship meet even though her one-hand touches and alternating leg kicks had disqualified her in every race.

Children, like Nelly, sometimes lack the confidence to race newly introduced events. Occasionally, the fear comes from nerves or from performing illegal strokes. I was waiting for it to click with Nelly. And then it happened. After a short pep talk, a fist bump and a smile, she dove in and started swimming butterfly—legally! Nelly finished to the wall with two hands! Out of six competitors in her heat, she placed . . . well, sixth.

In that moment, I couldn't contain my emotions. I cheered my lungs out for that girl. I expected her to be sad because she hadn't been a finalist or earned a medal. Eyes bright with pride, she ran to me.

"My mom said I placed sixth! That means I didn't get last." Technically, she hadn't. One person in the heat before her had been disqualified for touching the bottom of the pool and pulling on the lane lines.

"You did great," I exclaimed. "I'm so proud of you!"

Then, with a dramatic pause, she said, "This is the best day of my life!"

My heart bulged out of my chest. My eyes welled up. She hadn't won anything. It had taken all of her might and energy to swim the length of the pool. For me, swimming had always been about winning. Watching Nelly changed all that. She beamed with pride because she knew the juice was worth the squeeze. Her training, focus, and dedication paid off, and she was enthused to share the experience with me. For her, the moment meant so much more than conquering butterfly or being on a team. It was a confidence-builder, something she could hang her hat on. It was an accomplishment. Nelly created a poignant moment in my life as she expressed genuine emotion.

Sports do not build character. They reveal it.

***

To understand my motivation to become a swim coach requires additional information. I fell in love with sports immediately in life. Soccer and baseball, in addition to extracurricular activities, chewed up most of my time. Kicking a ball wasn't much fun unless the field was muddy. I couldn't hit a baseball to save my life. It was my friends that drew me in to team sports. The camaraderie and teamwork (not to mention the snacks after the game) motivated me to be there.

On my seventh birthday, my mother enrolled me in swim lessons at Orchard Hills, a local country club. The pool was a short walk from our home. I vividly remember walking with my mother to the pool as the warm sun beamed down. We'd cut through my second-grade teacher's lawn, which led down a big hill. I enjoyed swimming outdoors because being tan was cool.

My first swim coach was Mr. Campbell, an older man with silvery-white hair and a barrel chest. He taught physical education at a local school. During summer break, he passed the time by teaching swim lessons and managing the lifeguards. Mr. Campbell donned aviator sunglasses, sported a whistle that dangled loosely around his neck, and slicked his body with coconut-scented suntan lotion.

Mr. Campbell had us stretch before every swim lesson. The stretch was unnecessary for me because I was made of skin, bones, and whatever cereal I'd eaten that morning.

I was fearless in the water. My father was an avid boater, and he'd have us swimming in a lake or river almost every weekend. The water was my second home.

Mr. Campbell always started class in the shallow end of the pool. We eventually shifted over to the big lap lanes once everyone demonstrated a strong kick. I moved up a level the following season and became one of the stronger swimmers in the group. The year after that, I was officially part of the swim team, and I had a new swimsuit to prove it.

Swim meets were fun! Our coaches painted their faces and wore silly costumes to motivate and inspire us. We'd start each meet with a loud cheer. And when the meet was over, everyone ate pizza!

When you're good at something, you feel important. And when you're important, people notice you. The top swimmers in our area swam for the YMCA, and I noticed how fast they were in the summer. I yearned to be the best. At age 13, I joined the Powel Crosley Jr. YMCA swim team (not the same YMCA where I later volunteered; that one wasn't around yet). The move to year-round swimming, along with my parents' divorce, spread our family thin. Between the driving schedule and finances, swimming required commitment from everyone. Fortunately, we made it work.

The YMCA was thirty minutes from our home in Colerain Township. I didn't know many of the kids on the team, but they were friendly. As the new guy, I fit in because of my humor and playfulness. The majority of the swimmers only swam. I gave up all activities other than the cello to focus on swimming.

Playing the cello came naturally to me. I had an ear for music. My great uncles were musicians and my mother was a pianist. When I played the cello well, no one cheered loudly, but I felt accomplished. Musicians are a quiet bunch, whereas athletes make noise. My friends in orchestra thought I was a jock and my swimming friends thought I was Yo-Yo Ma. I identified with both groups.

On Wednesday nights, my mother shuttled me to orchestra practice nearly an hour away in Middletown, Ohio, where I met our fearless leader and conductor Doug Bruestle. I loved Doug. He had incredible leadership skills and was a member of our church. Doug was tall with a salt-and-pepper beard and a booming voice. I had two cello instructors and they were completely different from one another. Bob Aylesworth had me in middle school and Gerri Sutyak taught me throughout high school.

Bob, a gentleman in his seventies, hunched forward as he played the cello. He encouraged me to practice at home and have fun with music. We set up practice in a small room, and in the winter, it felt like I was playing on an iceberg. The draft in that room was absurd. Bob loved and supported me. He knew when to push me and when to coddle me.

Gerri was awesome but more boisterous than Bob. She often chided me for being a swimmer, but I knew where her heart was. She saw tremendous potential in me. She told me if I practiced Bach's Six Cello Suites more than my freestyle, I could get a scholarship for music and make it to New York. Gerri pushed me every second to be great. If I didn't play a song for her perfectly the first time, she made me do it five times more until it was better.

I'll always remember the long, steep gravel driveway that led up to her house. When I was late to practice, Gerri threatened to send me home. Her home was large and open, adorned with awards and pictures from her music career. As I played for her, she'd pace around the house, listening to my pitchy, screeching bow slide over the strings. If something wasn't right, it was because I swam. And if I played well, it was luck.

My first season swimming for the YMCA was difficult because of the doubles (morning and afternoon practices).The culture, being much different than my summer club program, changed the sport for me. Mike Leonard, the head coach of the Tigersharks, was the perfect leader because he cared and connected with his athletes at a higher level. He related to me through my first love—baseball. I idolized Will Clark of the San Francisco Giants. Before practice, we'd talk baseball, specifically Will's stats. Mike, along with Coach Sabrina King, kept me engaged and motivated.

The practices were tough. Swimming for a country club was one thing, but training at YMCA was another. I remember two hours of nonstop swimming as I missed every interval and send-off. Eventually, I improved. I moved to the front of the lane and qualified for the national team. I couldn't believe how far I'd come. My dedication paid off as I learned more about myself and my capacity to handle challenges.

I had one job in high school, which was easy, paid well, and provided flexibility around my practice schedule. Tom's Monfort Aquarium and Pets created the perfect role for me. I cleaned fish tanks and provided superior customer service to the patrons of the store. The owner, Tom, was a pleasant man with a teachable moment ready for me every day. He reminded me of Dennis Farina. Tom's customer service with hobbyists was top-notch. If the customer was extremely knowledgeable, he was ready for them. If the person was new to the hobby, he'd take them through the step-by-step process of aquarium setup. Every Friday evening, I'd clean algae off the aquarium glass with a razor blade. Tom made his rounds five minutes before my shift ended. I enjoyed his feedback on my work.

Swimming wasn't cool at my school. Football reigned supreme. I felt popular because I did something no one else did. My name was mentioned on the announcements a couple times. I held school records and that made me feel like one of the popular kids. At the end of my senior year, I quit cello. I decided I wanted to swim in college and didn't have time for music. I know the decision was hard for my mom and especially difficult for my grandmother.

Grandma Rose was everything to me. When my mother and father divorced, she moved in. A little addition was built on the back of our house. No one should be afraid of a five-foot, ninety-pound lady, but I was. Grandma Rose was straight from Armenia. If you think your upbringing was tough, you should have ten minutes with her. Rose and her siblings piled on a boat in Turkey and headed to Ellis Island. My grandmother, her brothers and sister didn't have anything. They didn't have money. They didn't know the language. But they had grit.

When they hit New York, they acted on instinct. One of her brothers made rugs, another was in music and filmmaking, and the other was good at everything. My grandmother was a survivor and a fighter. I don't know how she did it. She married my grandfather, Pete, and had an amazing marriage. My sister and I were left with Rose every day. She gave us discipline from sunup to sundown. I meticulously groomed the yard for her. I helped her make healthy meals. I cleaned every square inch of our house until it was dust-free. If I didn't do something up to her standards, I had to do it again the right way . . . right away. She loved listening to me play cello and I knew I made her happy. Before she died, she always told me I would miss her when she was gone. She was right. Grandma Rose was the best coach I ever had.

At the end of my senior year, I chose to attend the University of Cincinnati and swim for the Bearcats. Monty Hopkins became my coach, friend, and mentor. I remember the first phone call with him before I joined the team. He didn't tab me as one of his top recruits. I told him what I lacked in skill I'd make up in enthusiasm. The four years in college were full of fun. I tried to cherish every moment. I soaked up every laugh and high five. The training was intense. College made me a man. When I retired my goggles, the sport was out of my blood—or so I thought.

I graduated with a degree in dietetics, but I needed to do an internship to become a registered dietitian. Free labor was really what it was. I didn't want to jump into more school just yet and needed time to process the next life step. What should I do next? Should I power through and do the internship? Or, should I stay involved with swimming for one more year?

I applied for my first year-round coaching position in 1999.I put on a dark blue polo shirt, khaki pants, and shiny dress shoes for the interview. I met Brad Isham, the head coach for the Gamble-Nippert YMCA Gators, on a hot August afternoon. Brad was friendly and easygoing. The position was offered to me the next day. I'd become the assistant senior coach, having responsibility over the less-skilled high school swimmers and top age-group athletes. Brad and I had amazing success and Gamble-Nippert became the 2000 YMCA Long Course National Champions.

I needed to move forward with my dietetic career in 2000. Coaching wasn't paying the bills. Shortly after the summer season, I headed to Marshall University for my internship and graduate school. West Virginia was far different from Ohio.

West Virginia living was a slower but more enjoyable life for me. Marshall University provided the education I needed to excel in dietetics. I hiked, biked, and explored nature between and after classes. The nightlife was tame compared to what I'd had in Cincinnati. And, Marshall University had a pool. Since I'd gained a few pounds after college, I decided to swim three times a week. I felt great in the water, though I wasn't fit enough to complete long workouts.

After the internship, I decided to move back to Cincinnati. I went back to Gamble-Nippert YMCA for temporary employment until I found a job in dietetics, this time as a head coach. My first year at the helm turned out well. I was named Coach of the Year for the Southwest YMCA cluster in 2004.The following season, I received a call that would change my life forever.

The call came from an aquatic and programming director named Jennifer Mayer. She worked at a large local health system called Mercy Health. Mercy Health managed hospitals, long-term health-care facilities, and three health clubs with pools. Jen programmed the pools and wanted to start a swim team. She offered me a full-time position, complete with benefits and creative freedom. Gamble-Nippert had provided a wonderful base for me, but the opportunity couldn't have come at a better time.

I didn't know the first thing about starting a club, but I knew how to run one. Fifty athletes joined the Sea Wolves program during year one. In year two, we doubled in size. Over the next few years, two practice sites grew to three. I launched a masters swim program. I won my second award in 2009 when I was named Age Group Coach of the Year for Ohio Swimming. By year ten, we'd added 200 swimmers. Mercy accounted for multiple state record holders, high school champions, and athletes on the national stage. At one point, we were ranked 131st in the country. Nothing was more important than being a coach.

***

I've written about my childhood, my coaches, and the people who shaped my life.

Developing a team left little time to enjoy a social life. I was motivated to have the best team in the area, even if it meant sleeping in my office and neglecting my health.

A few years after the Sea Wolves launched, I met Sarah. She was introduced to me by a mutual friend I went to college with. Sarah understood me and was happy when I was happy. Most importantly, Sarah loved me at my best and at my worst. After three and a half years of dating, it was time to make our relationship official. I married her on April 2, 2011, in front of our family and friends.

Life moved fast. Six months later, as I shuffled in the front door of our small condo, Sarah had something to tell me. She looked down, glanced up, caught my eyes, and smiled. "We're pregnant!"

I hugged Sarah and dropped to my knees. My parents and sister heard the good news an hour later.

Sarah and I basked in excitement for the remainder of the week. The initial ultrasound appointment was scheduled the following Wednesday. So much was going through my mind. I yearned to be the best father alive. Sarah was feeling good. We found out we were having a girl! I was so excited! Our little darling kicked and moved around Sarah's belly constantly.

On Sarah's fourth doctor visit, something changed. We sat in a dark ultrasound room as the doctor and nurse whipped through images on the screen. The silence was eerie and uncomfortable. I sifted through emails on my phone as a much-needed distraction. As the ultrasound ended, the doctor and nurse slipped out into the hall without a word to us. I heard whispers and what sounded like a brief phone call. My stomach began to turn. The tone of the appointment had changed. Something was wrong. They entered the room as silently as they'd exited minutes before.

"Is everything okay?" I asked.

The doctor stood in front of us and spoke with a solemn tone. "We would like to take a closer look at your daughter's heart."

He referred us to a high-risk doctor the following week. The days that led up to the appointment were painful. What was wrong? Was our little girl in trouble?

Sarah and I held hands when we entered the hospital. She put on a gown for another ultrasound, the same way she did for previous visits. My feet were numb. My hands were cold. The specialist didn't speak much as he gelled up Sarah's belly. Images flashed up on the screen. I studied every black-and-white image. What was I looking for? After twenty minutes, the doctor gave a big sigh. He left the room for a brief minute and entered a moment later with a box of tissues. He looked directly into my eyes.

"Your daughter is sick. She has a rare congenital heart defect known as hypoplastic left heart syndrome (HLHS)."

I didn't hear anything else. Sarah and I embraced and we cried for hours. Our poor daughter was ill.

HLHS, simply put, is a malformation of the left side of the heart, which pumps oxygen-rich blood to the entire body. The right side of the heart is responsible for the lungs. An absence of the left heart puts tremendous pressure on the right side to send oxygen-rich blood to all organs and appendages. Without palliative care or surgery, infants with HLHS perish within the first hours of life. Sarah and I chose to move forward with the three-staged surgery that could save her life.

Corinne was born on April 4, 2012, just over a year after our wedding. She was beautiful, big, and full of life. Other than her cyanotic (blue) skin, you wouldn't know she was sick. She had six wires attached to her at all times. Machines beeped constantly. The nurses and doctors checked in hourly. My nerves were on edge from morning till night.

I felt Corinne's love shock my body when I held her. She was warm in my arms. Love doesn't describe it. The feeling was something stronger and more purposeful. Corinne progressed with each day. She tolerated her feedings and gained weight her first week in the CICU.

Sarah and I approached each day with trepidation because Corinne remained in critical condition. Within a week, she had her first surgery. She survived! Her weight and strength carried her through to recovery. Sarah stayed at the hospital day and night without sleep. She attended every meeting with the nurses and doctors, while I shuttled in and out of the hospital for work. Corinne had her mom at her bedside every day of her early life.

Days after Corinne's surgery, I had an anxiety attack in my office. I thought about my daughter's health and the hopelessness of the situation. I cried, paced back and forth, and chewed through my fingernails. The next day at practice, hopelessness turned into fear. The main set consisted of timed 25s from a push followed by active-recovery 50s. Our final group had just completed the timed 25s when an associate from our front desk barged in with panic on her face. "Aaron, call your wife quickly! We'll get someone to take practice! Get down to the hospital!"

My heart dropped and every ounce of breath left my lungs. I grabbed for my phone, but it wasn't in my front pocket. It was in my work bag, inexplicably set to vibrate. I had eight missed calls and four messages. Without hesitation, I raced down to the hospital.

Corinne had coded. I arrived while she was in surgery. The procedure was difficult for her. The staff added another monitor, more wires, and new tubes to my baby. Corinne was alive but gravely ill.

Sarah and I continued to stay by Corinne's bedside. We loved her recklessly for the remainder of her life on earth. Days after she coded, my beautiful daughter went back to her Heavenly Father.

Sarah and I struggled with the loss of Corinne. In fact, I hurt more today than I did then. I can't feel her warm skin now. I can't hear her little snorts when she naps. I savor the good memories without reliving the nightmarish moments.

Work was tough, too. The swim team rallied around us. Their love and strength helped. However, nothing cheered me up.

Months after Corinne passed, we headed up to Michigan for a weekend getaway. We stopped in a beach town just shy of Traverse City to use the bathroom and stretch our legs. I strolled down to the shore and stood next to three beached kayaks. A message was inscribed in the sand between two of the kayaks. It read, "I love you, Mom and Dad." A tear came to my eye. I looked around and no one else was within sight. Sarah joined me moments later. We were meant to stop. Sarah and I know when she is near, and on that day, she was with us.

Days later, my pastor stopped by for a brief visit. He was a nice man with a quirky sense of humor. After fifteen minutes of conversation, a bright yellow bird flew through the trees and landed on our porch railing. Yellow finches are somewhat common, but aren't often as radiant as this one. The bird remained there, unfazed by our presence, for another thirty minutes. I think it was Corinne checking in with her daddy. A vibrant yellow bird zips by every April now, and it's no coincidence.

Sarah and I had walked out of the hospital full of grief and sadness. Then, on a cool night just as our fall swim season commenced, Sarah revealed she was pregnant again.

We became the proud parents of a healthy baby boy named Rowan.

I found my groove again, thanks to the little man at home. The swim team grew and improved with each meet. We finished sixth at the Junior Olympic meet, our highest finish of all-time. The senior group traveled to Orlando for our first NCSA national meet in team history. National-level meets bring out the best in athletes. The swimmers at the meet didn't look like the athletes from back home. In fact, they didn't resemble our species. Every swimmer was bigger and stronger than the next!

The following season, I hired a talented coach named Brogan to assist with our senior-level group. He was from the area and had attended high school locally. The athletes loved Brogan. Our staff was better than ever.

Brogan and I were two peas in a pod. One fall, we drove up to Columbus, Ohio, for a swim meet one night early. He and I were hungry, but nothing healthy was available past ten on a weeknight. Brogan suggested we purchase a few frozen pizzas.

The night turned out better than I expected. I remember we tossed a football for a while at the hotel and followed it up with a fashion show. The manager warned us about the commotion we were causing. We headed to Wal-Mart, where Brogan bought three pizzas. I grabbed the desserts (cookies and ice cream) and we went back to the hotel.

Food coma came early. The next morning, we were ready to take on the state of Ohio at the Junior Olympic meet. Our team finished eighth in the state, with two of our athletes winning individual championships.

Two months later on a cool May morning, Brogan and I shared the pool deck one last time. He showed up to practice with his workout book tucked under his arm. The summer club season would kick off in a week, and I could tell he was excited.

The following day, Brogan was a no-show for our Sunday-afternoon practice. Our coaches reached out to him and didn't get a response. I contacted Brogan's cousin and his parents. No one had heard from him.

Hours went by. Days went by and there was no sign of Brogan.

Brogan's absence made the local and national news. Search teams combed the far corners of Ohio, Kentucky, and Indiana for a tall, slender boy with black-rimmed glasses. Fear infiltrated our minds. Where was he? Where had he gone? The police dropped by the pool to ask me about his disappearance. I thought about every conversation we'd had. I dissected our interactions, his mannerisms, and the overall mood. Brogan was Brogan. Nothing made sense.

A week later, I was reading a book in our basement. The murmur of the nightly news was on in the background. My phone, silenced only when I read or slept, buzzed. Then it buzzed again. A stream of texts flooded my screen. The national news station cut away to the local affiliate. Brogan's body had been recovered.

The next day, I gathered our swimmers to talk about Brogan's passing. I don't remember what I said, but my emotions were hard to suppress. The children and parents were devastated. He was a beautiful person, full of life. I think about him almost every day.

I had anxiety like I've never felt before. Our team went through a gauntlet of emotions. Between Corinne's passing, Brogan's death, and the birth of my son, I couldn't recover. I was sick most of 2014 with shingles, pneumonia, and asthmatic bronchitis.

We were blessed with the arrival of our daughter Eden in early 2015. Right from the start, Eden has been full of energy. Sarah held down the fort at home in addition to her full-time job. I continued to work crazy hours as a coach. Neither of us missed a beat. We encountered the normal, everyday challenges of life, but we loved it!

I bet you're asking: Why does all of this matter?

First, it's necessary to understand my perspective as both a coach and a parent. We're molded by the experiences we've had and thus become a new version of ourselves when we persevere through personal challenges and failures. Failure is the best teacher.

The second reason ties into the first. Effective coaches navigate through challenges and obstacles. The best coaches evolve and learn off-script. Coaches become more effective leaders on the road less traveled. Simply put, we must be agile.

The third reason connects to the previous two. Nothing can be accomplished without enthusiasm and passion. I love my family, friends, athletes, and colleagues. Not only do I love these people, but I learn from them. I learn to be passionate and enthusiastic with everything I pursue. There are teachable moments everywhere.

The final reason is significant. Events that have impacted you will impact others. Coaches and teachers are the most influential people (outside of family) an athlete will cross paths with. We build confidence, self-esteem, drive, and determination. We introduce goal setting and teach valuable life skills. And we encourage athletes to take massive action in the pool and become better swimmers.

My objective for this book is simple: I aim to usher swim coaches through the refined process of team management. In some areas, the details are specific, and in others, I take a broader approach. Take notes, process the information, self-reflect, and enjoy!

Chapter 2: Coaching Is a Privilege

As you know, being a coach is an appreciable honor and privilege. I've never thought of coaching as a career. I once read that a perfect career is the marriage of passion and discipline. If it feels like work, you have a job. If it feels like excitement, then you have a career.

My need to coach is intrinsic, much like DNA codes hair and eye color. Coaches derive energy from athletes after a great performance. Athletes gain strength from our mentorship. The connection between the two is seamless synergy.

Coaches challenge swimmers to overcome objections, barriers, and painful sets. Have you come up with a long set just to see who will fight for it? We want to see character over talent. We want to see leadership evolve within our team.

I learn something new every year. Last year, I challenged myself to be more forgiving with the season plan—in other words, to be creative on the fly. It bothered me. However, I can't evolve and improve unless I go through self-reflection. After all, athletes are looking for leadership. If I don't improve, their ability to grow in life and the sport of swimming ends in a necrotic mess.

Life as a swim coach is not a perfect science. Be agile, embrace leadership, show patience, and eat a slice of humble pie every once in a while. I won't tell you how to do your job. But have an open mind and create space for new ideas. Coaching is fun and certainly a privilege.

Chapter 3: I'm the Coach

The first word on the other end of the phone came through loud and clear.

"Congratulations!"

Jen Mayer, my soon-to-be supervisor, had called to extend me an offer. My heart was beating so fast I couldn't catch my breath. Luckily, she continued to speak.

"We're pleased to name you the new head coach of the Mercy swim team. We have you starting at the beginning of September, so you'll need to assemble a staff. Also, we ask that you get your marketing piece and pricing to the front desk as soon as possible. So, what will you need from us to get started?"

In 2004, I was hired to build a team from the ground up. Jen, who was cautiously optimistic when she brought me on, thought a nice pool in an affluent area would yield instant success. On the first day of employment, I sat in my newly furnished office in shock. I kept repeating to myself, "I'm the coach." I'd just taken on the biggest task of my life and didn't know where to begin.

Before you hire coaches, establish team fees, develop marketing pieces, or write a season plan, you must establish team culture. Culture defines your team and is an extension of your character. High-character coaches emphasize the importance of a culture in which everyone is heard, respected, trusted, and supported. The head swim coach upholds this with his or her associates, athletes, and swim parents. Team goals and objectives cascade down from culture.

Exceptional team culture grows from a strong, ethical environment. Coaches set the standards. Make sure you put these in place immediately. Identify the pillars of cultural success for your team. I carried these pillars with me everywhere I went: Treat everyone with respect, be punctual, be supportive of teammates, be coachable, and be gracious.

Culture shouldn't be exclusive; it should be inclusive. I once heard a coach say he *only* brought on swimmers who felt the same way he did. It was no surprise to me that his team never improved. Culture isn't about like-mindedness.

When you're hired in a new role as I was, there's excitement around the program. We gained interest in what we were doing. A prominent swimmer from another club team reached out to me. She wanted to join our team because, in her words, she "wasn't getting better." I set up a meeting with her family. Both her mom and dad were pleasant. As I spoke, they took notes, asked questions, and were incredibly engaged.

I paused at the end of my pitch and asked, "How do you feel about what you've heard?"

The fourteen-year-old responded. "Do you give more attention to your top athletes? I'd be one of your top girls, correct?"

I minded her response and replied. "I give each swimmer my very best. Each athlete is entitled to a high level of respect. A hierarchy of care does not exist within the framework of our team."

I sensed her uneasiness in the way her body language changed. "I'm one of the top swimmers on my team. My coach focuses on my goals and works with me personally. . . you know, because I score the most points."She sighed. Under her breath, she muttered, "Well, I guess I'll stay where I'm at."

I thanked her for the visit. The best teams aren't talent-collection agencies. Adding "just anyone" negatively impacts the morale and the culture of a team.

My next anecdote pertains to culture, but it occurred several years after our team was established.

We traveled to Indiana for a big meet in the summer of 2012. Our team area was adjacent to that of another club twice our size. Their warm-up time was seven thirty a.m. I looked at my watch at seven thirty-five. Athletes were playing on their phones, reading books, and looking disengaged. Then, their head coach stood up (apparently he'd lost track of time) and yelled, "Get in the water! Everyone, get in the water!" For the remainder of the weekend, I monitored his behavior. I peered over periodically. He was glued to his chair. He played on his phone. He ignored his swimmers after races. He'd leave the deck and smoke cigarettes. I was embarrassed for his athletes.

As the meet ended, he walked over and sat on our bench. He wanted to talk. "Kids don't understand what it takes to be good at this sport. My guys are a bunch of losers. I can't wait to get out of this meet."

Fortunately, it was the last time this so-called coach graced us with his presence. He was terminated a month later. Great coaches model appropriate behaviors if they want their athletes to follow suit.

I firmly believe implanting a successful team culture starts with a written plan. The plan specifically defines roles, behavior, training philosophy, and process. Process is important. I have a process for everything within our club structure. Here's an example.

To train with our team, athletes have to successfully complete an evaluation test set. We explain the process and address the "Why." Parents and athletes learn the process. The purpose is to group similarly skilled and appropriately aged athletes together.

Define roles and behaviors within your club; this is essential for synergy. Assistant coaches make or break a team's reputation in the community. Evaluate each coach and his or her role. Is the coach the right fit for the assignment? Does the coach embrace your coaching philosophy and style? Assistant coaches are creative followers and leaders. Coaches align their process around the team framework with a creative twist.

Coaching philosophy is the offshoot of culture. Philosophy is style harmoniously tied to outlook. For example, use a statement to define your outlook, such as: "We train for all strokes and all distances."

Define your training philosophy with the preeminent team goal in mind. Philosophy is a matter of fact. I've used a statement such as this: "We want our athletes to peak at championships."

Never embellish your philosophy. Never overpromise and under-deliver. Philosophy should be true to you.

Address discipline with culture. I point the finger at myself for not being stronger here. Culture is black and white with a sliver of gray. Either you support an ideal or you don't. Handle problems and concerns with your team in a consistent fashion. Create a policy handbook with specific rules. Define a discipline to correlate with each infraction. Policy handbooks are helpful, healthy for club culture, and provide transparent information to families. Be aware of athlete behavior outside of the pool. The sliver of gray applies here.

The head coach standardizes a policy for dress code, hygiene, behavior, and social media. Engage coaches weekly with touch-base meetings. In these meetings, share ideas and keep them in the loop with changes. I'll talk more about assistant coaches in chapter eight.

Chapter 4: Goal-Setting

Coaches create challenging yet attainable goals for their team. Goals are the long-term plans for the program and intrinsically align with leadership. Everyone fights for the team goals, including your assistant coaches, who will set goals for their respective groups.

Failure is inevitable. Part of becoming a more effective leader is evaluating the motives and processes behind your goals. I've questioned everything in our program at least once.

- Why are we losing athletes to our competitors?

- Why do we have 75 percent practice attendance and 60 percent meet attendance?

- Why aren't we a top-100 program?

- What do I need to change about my coaching style?

As a novice coach, I was afraid to evaluate myself. Self-exploration and self-reflection can be excruciating.

In addition to these tough questions, I made a list of thoughts focused on growth mindset.

- Will inter-brand shadowing opportunities allow us to become better coaches?

- What can I do to increase brand recognition?

- Are summer club clinics the most efficient use of time when marketing our program?

If you're comfortable with self-evaluation, you'll have a program of excellence.

Short-term steps that are date-sensitive and actionable build strategy for goal achievement.

- Goal: Double the size of our 11-to-14 age group by this date next year (you may choose the date and year to make it specific).

- Action step one: Provide a free clinic to each summer club within ten miles of our location in June.

- Action step two: Send a flyer home with every child graduating from swim lessons by August.

Focus on one or two goals around your coaching staff. Goals for your coaches maintain accountability and discipline through the season plan. Meet with coaches weekly to review and analyze test-set results. Send coaches to a clinic in the fall and have them create a presentation for the staff based on the experience. These strategies increase retention because they engage your staff at a higher level. When your staff is engaged, they'll feel responsible for the growth of the team. Additional subjects for goals are practice attendance, meet attendance, and feedback analysis from parent satisfaction surveys. Track your success. Are you following the action steps to achieve your goal? If you don't track, you don't grow.

Accounting for variables is necessary in goal setting. Coaches control the controllable. One way to do it is through a team performance goal. I send an email to coaches the night before Junior Olympics encouraging them to pump up the swimmers in their group. These emails created a stir within our staff, and they worked!

Create goals focusing on success and growth. Be aggressive with objectives and take massive action every day. The plan won't be perfect by any means, but it provides a platform to build on.

Chapter 5: Registration, Practice Scheduling, and Meet Selection

Registration is handled by an assistant coach, team manager, treasurer, volunteer, or board member. Head coaches supervise the process. The board, along with input from the head coach, formulates a reasonable fee structure for each group. Team fees are based on financial goals and market value.

Account for all costs and expenses of your program when determining your dues. Expenses include salary, travel, office supplies, deck equipment, team functions, rentals, and technology. Nonprofit programs set team dues to offset their expenses. For-profit entities need to yield a specific percentage over cost because of their particular situation (most likely a partnership with a medical-based facility or school).

The next point, mostly pertaining to market value, is more subjective. Ask these questions when setting the registration fees:

- What's our market share for the community?

- Are seasonal swimmers choosing our program over other teams?

- Do we have the best team in our primary market?

- Have we added new technology to support our coaches, swimmers, and families?

- Can we charge more for our program and get the same enrollment?

I've occasionally priced my team out of a market. However, we offered more value, coaching consistency, and schedule flexibility than other programs in the marketplace. Registration fees cover the bulk of the major expenses. The remainder is covered by fundraising and hosting meets. If you add programs to enhance athletic performance, factor it in with registration. Return on investment (ROI) is a key data point. Develop a process to monitor the efficacy of value-added programs. Yoga classes, a personal trainer, or a registered dietitian are investments that add value to swim teams and will increase engagement.

I shop my competitors for pricing information. Most teams put their pricing online. Never put the registration form online. Families get turned off by it, normally, because the cost of the program is more than they budgeted for. Car dealerships call this "sticker shock." A family with genuine interest is sold on the value of your program, not the price. Sell your staff's coaching quality (years of experience, coaching clinics attended, etc.). Promote the air quality of the pool (new HVAC, filtration devices, etc.). Talk quality before price. Learn to overcome objections.

Prorate dues for families playing other sports or taking part in activities, and be cautious of families trying to abuse your policy. Set rules for prorating and make sure your board and supervisor are in agreement with the policy.

Capture as much information as you can during the registration process. If you host an open house, have a sign-in table with a volunteer or assistant coach welcoming your guests. Follow up with families via an email, note, or phone call. Thank them for stopping by and get as much feedback from them as you can.

***

Practice schedules are time-consuming and challenging to develop. Scheduling pool time is the biggest obstacle for me. The plethora of uncontrollable variables draws out the process and frustrates my colleagues because they want the schedule to be correct on the first draft. Therefore, I came up with a process to streamline scheduling.

Swim team ABC consists of 100 athletes and four coaches. The 10-and-younger group has twenty athletes, the 11-and-12 age group has thirty athletes, the 13-and-14 age group has forty athletes, and the senior group has ten athletes. Each of the four coaches leads a group. The coach leading the 10-and-younger athletes assists the 13-and-14 lead coach on weekdays. As the head coach, your strategy is to have five practices a week available for everyone under the age of 15 and six practices open for those 15 and older. The youngest group has a one-hour practice. With each ascending tier comes an additional half hour. The upper group's practices are two and a half hours and occasionally include dryland or weights. The pool is a six-lane, 25-yard pool. Mondays and Wednesdays you have the pool from five o'clock till eight thirty p.m. On Tuesdays and Thursdays, you have the pool from five to nine p.m. On Fridays, you have the pool from four o'clock until eight thirty p.m. Saturdays, the availability is a little more challenging. The pool is open from eight to eleven thirty a.m., but only three lanes are available from ten o'clock until eleven thirty. In addition, you have space at a local fitness club in their 20-yard warm-water pool from ten to eleven a.m. with two lanes. The stage is set.

Scheduling is a daunting task when you're dealing with numbers like these. Keep your poise and be patient. I start scheduling with the least flexible group. In this case, we're focused on the 10-and-younger athletes. Consider travel, school dismissal, dinner and additional commitments with the little ones. I've given us an easy example. Here is what I see:

10-and-younger athletes: Monday, Tuesday, and Thursday five to six p.m. (two lanes). Fridays seven to eight p.m. Saturdays ten to eleven a.m. at the fitness club (two lanes). Based on history and practice attendance, I expect fourteen athletes per practice on weekdays and a dozen on Saturdays. Weekends tend to be busy for our athletes due to other sports, family outings, and cartoon watching. Athletes in this age group will come three times a week. The off day is Wednesday.

The times are reasonable. The weekdays are late enough to get to practice from school and still make it to dinner. Saturday at the fitness club works well. The little ones tend to have less body fat. With a warmer, shorter pool, you can work on technique.

The 11-and-12 group is next. These athletes rely on parents to shuttle them around. I'd expect to see an average of four practices a week or approximately 75 percent attendance.

11 and 12s: Monday, Tuesday, Wednesday, and Friday, five to six thirty p.m. (three lanes). Saturdays: ten to eleven thirty a.m. (two lanes). Thursdays will be an off day.

The 13 and 14 age group is our largest group. They will need four lanes for safety and size. These athletes attend more practices than younger swimmers. Due to the size of the group, we need help from another assistant coach.

13 and 14s: Mondays, Wednesdays, and Fridays, six thirty to eight thirty p.m. (four lanes). Thursdays: six to eight p.m., sharing with the senior group for thirty minutes. Saturdays: eight to ten a.m. (four lanes). Tuesdays are the day off. The 10-and-under coach helps with this group during the week. Saturdays are lighter and the practice expectation is 80 percent.

The schedule for the senior group is a standard six-day routine. Due to their size, training routine, and the need for more specific training, pool space is essential.

15 and older: Mondays, six thirty to eight thirty p.m. (they will share with another group for thirty minutes). Tuesdays: six to eight p.m. (two lanes). Wednesdays and Thursdays: seven to nine p.m. (two lanes with dryland thirty minutes before practice). Fridays are four to six p.m. (two lanes or more at most times). Saturdays are eight to ten a.m. (two lanes) with dryland following water training. I enjoy training older athletes on Saturday mornings. It prepares them for early morning prelim/final meets.

Teams in excess of 100 swimmers crowd a standard six-lane pool. When lanes become crowded, the quality of a program significantly decreases. Moreover, safety is compromised.

When your team shares pool space with recreational swimmers at a YMCA or health club, managing lanes is like putting together a 500-piece puzzle. I didn't want to frustrate our general manager by taking more lanes away from the recreation swimmers than I needed to. I developed a spreadsheet of our team's practice attendance, the number of swimmers per group, the swimmers per hour per lane, and the number of coaches per group. Data gives you leverage and gains the trust of the people in charge of scheduling. I presented the general manager these statistics in 2012.

- We max out eight average-sized 12-and-younger athletes per lane, seven average-sized 13 to 14 year olds per lane, and six average-sized 15-and-older athletes per lane.
- 10 and younger practice attendance = 67% (40 total children for 2012)
  11 and 12 practice attendance = 71% (35 total children for 2012)
  13 and 14 practice attendance = 77% (30 total children for 2012)
  15 and older practice attendance = 88% (30 total children for 2012)

We needed three lanes per group per the practice attendance percentage.
- Our average swimmer per lane per hour on a busy weekday was 7.3 in 2011.
- We had one coach per group in 2011. I convinced my supervisor to add another coach for our youngest groups for safety and efficient technique instruction.

Practice schedules are organized by group, age, skill, and coaching coverage. If you're making changes to schedules due to holidays, school closings, etc., create an addendum and send it out in a timely manner.

***

Creating a meet schedule is exciting for a head coach. We seek out challenging competition for our athletes but are fiscally responsible in the process.

When developing a meet schedule, have a short, specific list of facility requirements. I schedule meets lacking warm up/warm-down lap lanes and poor starting blocks early in the season so my athletes can adjust to an imperfect setting. We attend meets with warm pools, small team areas, and poor spacing between events. Challenge your athletes to be agile and overcome objections.

Midseason rest and full taper meets are scheduled at deep, well-lit pools. Each venue has a warm-up/warm-down area with ample deck space. Many times, I put a prelims/finals meet on the schedule at a university or college pool. Travel meets are fun for athletes. Swimmers bond on the road and learn how to become responsible for their activities of daily living.

Don't avoid travel to save money and cut expenses. National competitions improve brand recognition for the program and your athletes. Find a way to raise the money or budget it into team fees. One of my colleagues didn't attend the NCSA championship meet in Orlando because his board voted against it. Money was the determining factor. His team consisted of 200 athletes and qualified eight athletes to the meet. The board focused on the immediate financials instead of the opportunity to create fans. Just by publicizing meet attendance and performance over social media, the team attracts a handful of clicks from prospective swimmers. How many athletes would join his team knowing they might attend a meet in Florida annually? Would NCSAs increase athlete engagement and practice attendance if this meet is on the schedule? And, will athletes leave the team for another one if they attend this meet? Penny-pinching boards and frugal coaches lose swimmers when opportunities for travel are limited.

I enjoy having parents travel with the team. When I was a young coach, I had my fair share of travel meet challenges. Athletes violated curfew, lit animals on fire (true story), and ended up in the rooms designated for the opposite sex. There are advantages of team travel. USA Swimming registered parent chaperones add value to team travel. Chaperones act as your travel agent, chauffeur swimmers to and from the pool, order and serve meals, set up team dinner reservations, and help you maintain your sanity. The number-one priority is keeping your athletes safe and ready for competition. Team travel provides the development of strong interpersonal relationships and a higher level of trust among teammates.

Chapter 6: How to Launch and Execute a Season Plan

Club coaches are creatures of habit and, whenever possible, avoid radical changes. Swimmers evolve and change based on how coaches evolve and change. Review your season plan, action steps, and initiatives before the season starts. Self-reflect specifically within the areas of growth, evolution, and balance.

Areas of Importance (With Sample Action Steps and Initiative)

- Overarching Team Goal: Become a Silver Medal Team per USA Swimming's competencies.
- Strengthening the Weaknesses: Improve overall team technique by having a video session and review every Friday.
- Strengthening the Strengths: Continue to spend one morning per week focused on speed and power.
- Maintaining Amazing Culture: Organize a team breakfast after the first Saturday-morning practice of each month to foster the feeling that the team is a family.
- Growth Mindset and Strategy: Add a peer coaching session the Monday after each swim meet to review performance.
- Empowering the Staff: Ask coaches to submit an idea once a month to help grow the program.
- Enabling the Resources: Utilize the dive well to work on short-burst sprinting twice per week.
- Adding the "One New Thing" (ONT) for This Year: Schedule a week-long training trip over the holiday break to refocus athletes for the final leg of the season.

Allow athletes and swim parents to view your plan. Transparency is the goal; it cuts down on the communication you'll have to provide as the season unfolds.

Commence the season and practices on a positive note. Positivity begins with the first practice. Inferior coaches write a warm-up on the board, point to the set, sit in a chair, and count down the minutes until practice is over. Athletes won't respond positively to this. Great coaches are attentive and engage athletes from the first minute they show up. Start with genuine conversations about school, activities, or pop culture. Write the warm-up on the board, but put a quote underneath it (or a question of the day). Nominate an athlete to be "lane hero" or captain for the week. Come up with a competitive activity before the athletes get in the water. Lead an active warm-up. Whatever it is, do something fun and engaging.

I care about and connect with my athletes. Athletes ask questions. Is it a quality day? Are we doing a kick set today? Answer those questions to build rapport and trust. Most importantly, get them in on time. Be active during the warm-up and warm-down. Great coaches never sit for practice (unless they have a physical ailment). Don't play on your phone and never have an extended conversation with anyone on deck other than an athlete or coach.

I'll talk to the assistant coaches after swimmers start warm-up. I'll address their role and responsibilities for the day. Typically, assistants add value by taking splits, documenting stroke rates, motivating athletes, or videotaping. Each athlete receives communication from a coach throughout the practice. Athletes want to feel your energy. I'm a fist-bumper and high-fiver. I jump around when a swimmer has a great practice. Provide feedback to all athletes. At the end of the workout, huddle, do a break, or give a short motivational talk. Close each practice with energy.

Premier coaches use periodization and training cycles to support the season goal. I separate the seven-month fall/winter season into five parts. The first part is the adaptation phase. Here, I focus on body position, balance, flexibility, and overall nonspecific fitness. I maintain this phase for four to six weeks. Staples of adaptation are drill, kick (we kick for 25 percent of our practices), and pull with paddles for proper arm angle and body position. Hardwiring championship behavior starts here.

The second phase is skill development. After establishing a firm base in adaptation, I'll separate athletes based on physiological factors. Of course, this is mainly subjective. In a larger group with a small pool, specificity (training athletes by physiology) with basic methodology is a challenge. I'd be a more successful coach with eight wide lanes instead of six narrow ones. However, never complain about what you have. Bad coaches make excuses. Good coaches make exceptions. Great coaches make it happen, regardless of what they have. Be agile.

Why do coaches need to be agile? Well, let's look at lanespace. Coaches with limited space tend to be more agile and creative than those with plenty of space. With limited space, coaches run stations, initiate split squads (one group does dryland and one group is in the pool), and perhaps increase kicking on high-attendance days to reduce the risk of injury from spinning arms. Programs with prime pool time and space separate from the pack. Space is an advantage.

Within skill development, we harness strengths. Sprinters refine speed from their fast glycolytic and ATP-PC energy systems. They focus on dynamic skills through ten-yard bursts with cords, sprints with tennis balls, and jumps off the bottom of the pool. Distance-oriented swimmers adapt to fast aerobic swimming. In this energy system, coaches develop longer snorkel swims at submax pace and pull sets with a focus on efficiency and stroke rate with a Tempo Trainer.

Four to six weeks of skill development is optimal for all swimmers, but the concepts from this phase are peppered in daily. Never omit skill development from a training cycle.

After skill development, we load. The majority of coaches load for a certain period of time and follow it up with recovery. Recovery comes as a rest week or a "shake-out" day. The goal within the season is to keep swimmers healthy and avoid injury. Load is both objectively and subjectively created based on goals. For sprinters, incorporate more power work on loose intervals. With distance swimmers, develop a string of 100s on a tight interval. I've added a set (in short-course yards) of 75s at 100 goal pace followed by 175s at 200 goal time.

Athletes reveal their grit during the load phase. Incorporate something every day to create mental toughness within your swimmers. Four-day meets wear swimmers down. Prelim and final meets hurt. Do everything in your power to challenge your athletes. If you overload your athletes, make sure the extra yardage serves a purpose. Don't confuse overload with garbage yardage. Make everything count.

Specification occurs after the load phase. Each set has a purpose. Athletes focus on specificity versus a generic outcome. A keen focus on speed and dynamic movement is important. Mid-distance swimmers focus on pace goals with tight intervals. The sprinters work 25s at 50 or 100 pace with soft intervals. In our program, sprinter yardage dropped 30 percent from the previous phase but the distance and IM group stays static or increases by 10 percent. I like to push the legs with timed kick sets during specification, mostly in body position. Athletes in this phase are consistently achieving pace goals within the appropriate heart rate range. At least once during this two-week to four-week period, athletes wear a tech suit for timed swims in practice.

The final phase of our training is taper. Taper length, quality, and volume are important. Coaches consider kinesiology, physiology, anatomy, gender, grit, yardage, and persona when creating a successful taper program. When coaches face a lack of pool time and space, this phase can be a chore. Do the best you can with what you have. Set up a goal meeting with each athlete before taper. Taper displays what our athletes have done, not what they haven't done. The thoughts in this table are more to the rule and not the exception.

TAPER	Taper Start Yardage	Weeks of Taper	Drop in Yardage (%) per Week	Number of Timed Swims on Watch in Final Week	Notes: Keep Volume With Swimmers Who Race More Than Four Prelim Races
Male Sprinter	6,000	3-3.5	20%-25%	4 Sprints,1-2 Pace	High Grit = More Shake-out Swimming
Female Sprinter	6,000	2.5-3	15%-20%	4 Sprints, 3-4 Pace	High Grit = More Shake-out Swimming
Male IM/Mid-D	6,500	2.5-3	15%-20%	3 Sprints,4-5 Pace	Work Pace Weak IM leg/3rd 50s of IM
Female IM/Mid-D	6,500	2-2.5	10%-15%	3 Sprints, 5-6 Pace	Work Pace Weak IM leg/3rd 50s of IM
Male Distance	7,000-7,500	2-2.5	10%-15%	8-10 Pace Swims	Work Both Even and Goal Pace 50s/100s
Female Distance	7,000-7,500	1.5-2	5%-10%	10-12 Pace Swims	Work Both Even and Goal Pace 50s/100s

Communicate the goals for the season plan to your athletes on a regular basis. Create a forum to discuss the plan and encourage feedback. Athletes on our team can view the season plan at any time. I maintain a hard copy of the plan on my desk and a working document on my laptop. Throughout the season, I critique the plan. Sometimes, things go well. Other times, the plan fails. Failure is just another opportunity to learn. Evaluate the plan weekly, if not daily.

One season, I wrote a main set that started as two times a 600 specialty on a soft interval followed by a string of 6 x 100s best average. I had us doing it six times. The goal was to deplete our athletes through aerobic swimming and then challenge them with tempo repeats. By the fourth round, the swimmers were sloppy and technique was atrocious. Butterfliers and backstrokers weren't kicking off walls. Breaststrokers couldn't get past the flags on pullouts. What was the purpose of the set? Did I want to beat the athletes to a pulp or provide quality reps at a higher heart rate?

After practice, I went to my office and fidgeted for ten minutes. What was the long-term goal of the set and did it align with my season plan? I put pen to paper and changed the set. A month later, we tried the new and improved set. I changed the 600s to 300s freestyle pull for variety. I loosened the send-off times for the 100s and gave athletes the option to do a 50 at 100 pace for one rep each round. Watch and listen to your athletes. By doing this, you'll evolve as a coach.

Training is a grind. Athlete engagement is the key to a healthy and successful season plan. Take every opportunity to make swimming fun. I spoke to a few high-profile coaches and asked them how they incorporate fun in training.

One coach allows athletes to write a set for the last fifteen minutes of Friday workouts. Her rationale is simple: Athletes enjoy competition and teamwork. The team created Friday fun-day relays. Athletes dumped their mesh bags out and organized the equipment behind two lanes. The lead-off swimmers for each relay tied a mesh bag around their legs close to the ankle. Each swimmer was to race a 50, place a piece of equipment in the bag, untie the bag, and then tie it on to another swimmer. The process went on until all equipment was bagged up. Athletes exhausted themselves as they pulled five to ten pounds of equipment behind them. She said her group looked forward to the challenge.

Another coach incorporated fun with music. The swimmer who shows the most improvement on a test set gets to play music of their choice in practice. He allows the swimmer to choose a song to sing (and they can miss an entire set doing karaoke). I bet they have fun doing this!

The final coach I spoke to allows her athletes to play water whiffle ball during Saturday practices. Swimmers use a kickboard to bat. Athletes swim from base to base (ladders are first and third base with a dive block as second base in the middle of the pool) with short burst sprints. The losing team swims a 500 butterfly without breaking stroke as punishment.

The execution of a season plan through practice is a fun and rewarding experience. Develop tools to keep your athletes engaged.

Chapter 7: Taper Time

Taper isn't a perfect science. Create a taper program with confidence. Take your past experience, mix it with a little science, and add conviction. It doesn't hurt to learn more about physiology, kinesiology, and psychology.

I adhere to personal experience and basic science with taper. Getting too "cute" with taper confuses swimmers and complicates the process. The best coaches maintain a clear pathway and partnership with their athletes throughout the taper. If your swimmer thinks he or she is doing too much in practice the day before a meet, have a conversation. If your swimmer wants to do more pace work, have a conversation. Actively participate in the taper by being positive and encouraging. Wear a smile on your face every day and do some reflection after each practice.

"When do we taper?"

Taper time is fun, but sometimes you get sick and tired of the question. Athletes are rowdy and obnoxious during taper. In the end, it's worth it.

A successful taper pulls in multiple factors.

(Preparation + Realized Goals + Maximized Skill Set) x Confidence = Excellent Taper!

- Taper works if the athlete has worked. Fast swimming isn't magical or luck. Great performance is born from dedication, discipline, and accountability. I track data on my athletes as a way to develop a better taper. The chart has two sets of information. One contains objective information on attendance, test set times, weight room activity, meet performance, and total training yardage. On the other side of the chart, I have subjective information. The subjective portion specifically focuses on accountability, discipline, dedication, determination, technique, attitude, heart, and grit. With each area, I use a scoring system from one to five (with one being poor and five being outstanding). The goal is to average a four across the board. I made my log accessible to swim parents.

- The sudden or gradual drop in yardage, mixed with the looser intervals, breathes life into your athletes. Instill more confidence in your athletes by providing these three components. One is pace work on a watch. Pace is a confidence-builder for both you and the athlete. I provide pace goals based on goal times. Variations in pace are great for swimmers. Challenge athletes to hit their third 50 of a 200 or achieve an even goal pace. Mix up pacing with "to a turn" versus "to a touch." I won't yell out times if a swimmer suffers from meet anxiety. Analysis equals paralysis. The second essential component is stroke rate. Establish a goal stroke rate for races. Have an assistant coach call out stroke rate as you're evaluating effort and technique. The final component to increase confidence in taper are fins. Fins are necessary for "over speed" training. Confidence increases with speed work.

- Drop yardage with discretion. Most coaches are afraid to "over rest" an athlete. Tapers can last up to a month, but the decline in yardage from day to day will vary. My thoughts on this are spelled out in a chart from an earlier chapter.

  - In general, females can stay up in yardage as long as they buy in and understand why they're doing it.

  - Give sprinters more rest (up to two weeks) over their distance-swimming counterparts. These athletes stay at a low volume, specifically over the five to seven days leading up to the meet. "Drop dead" sprinters can do a meet warm-up the day before championships and are ready to go. Aerobic swimmers should keep volume up by performing sets that elevate the heart rate. Monitor heart rate on distance swimmers, particularly when they're incorporating pace within a set.

  - Do the math. Our athletes complete 5,500 to 7,500 yards in a two-hour practice. In a typical day of competition, an athlete can hit

2,500 to 3,000 yards (this includes warm-up, a few races, and a light shake-out after each swim). I won't take my athletes far under this total heading into a longer championship meet. I'm not impressed with coaches who squeeze one or two days of fast swimming out of an athlete. The Olympics, trials and nationals are competitions greater than three days. Prepare your athletes for a tremendous taper. Undertraining athletes forces them to scratch swims at championships and fall apart at finals. How can athletes be successful at a three-day championship meet when they swim more in a prelim/final meet than they would at a practice? Be smart with your athletes and set them up for long-term success.

- Play with toys in taper. During taper, increase over-speed training and quickness. Cords (walk out/race in with deck assist from teammates), fins, and diving boards are tools to incorporate dynamic swimming. One team in Florida has their athletes carefully jog down a diving board, launch with one bounce and race to the other side of the pool. I'm not opposed to using buckets, weighted kickboards, and parachutes during taper, just as long as your athletes are explosive when working with them.
- Be strong during taper. With sprinters, I back off strength training two weeks before the meet and then cut it off altogether five days before competition. Distance swimmers continue lifting light through taper, often up to three days before the meet. Maintaining strength training during taper is crucial.
- Visualization is a creative way to get swimmers ready for the meet. Athletes find success and win the race with self-visualization. Scrimmaging races before physically competing, without expending additional energy, alleviates distress heading into a championship meet.

- Coaches and swimmers won't miss taper by a day but they will miss it by a season.

"Hey coach, you missed my taper!"

If you've heard this, I bet it was difficult not to take it personally. Taper is a window of time versus a fleeting moment of success, which is contrary to what many believe. Swimmers put the time and work in to yield an amazing taper. Years ago, one of my top swimmers left us for a rival club. The reason for her departure was due to my taper plan. She felt she was being over-tapered. Months after her departure, I checked in with her new coach. She was attending six practices a week (including all offered dryland sessions) and had quit her other activities to focus on swimming. With our team, her attendance was 62.5%. Now, she was over 90%. She did well at champs, and some thought I was upset about it. I wasn't. A taper works when the athlete does.

- Coaches evaluate in-season performance meets as a way to provide more or less taper for the championship meet.
- Taper brings a crowd. At our pool, we call this the "taper phenomenon." Coaches see an uptick in attendance when taper begins. The pool is full, lane lines bow, and the noise doubles. Parents send their kids to more practices than they did before. Twice as much yardage in the pool makes a swimmer even more tired. We end up working them twice as hard instead of resting them more. Educate your athletes on taper. Taper starts on day one of the season and not two weeks out from championships.

The equation at the start of this chapter is the best way to conceptualize taper. Part one is preparation. Coaches focus on practice attendance, work ethic, motivation, and attitude. À la carte essentials such as stretching, ice baths, a healthy diet, sleeping, rolling out, meditation, yoga, and massage add to success. High performers put an emphasis on everything. The second component in the equation is a realized goal. A realized goal is created and carried out by the athlete. Coaches usher athletes through the process of goal realization. The third part of the equation is imperative. In 2009, I had the honor to coach four talented 11- to 12-year-old girls. These four girls set the Ohio Junior Olympic meet record in the 200 medley relay. Each girl maximized her own skill set. Sadie, our backstroker, had amazing underwaters. The flexibility in her ankles and hips carried her fifteen meters off every wall. Jess, our breaststroker, possessed an incredible kick. Paired with impeccable timing, she was the best breaststroker in the pool. Mikka, our butterflier, effortlessly slipped through the water. She stayed low in the water and made the most out of her frame. Our anchor, Julia, wanted to win more than anyone in the pool. The "rooster tail" created by her powerful kick separated her from the field. They maximized their talent and capitalized on their "superpowers" to win the race and set a meet record. Confidence, when multiplied by each ingredient, can transform an athletic performance from good to great. Without confidence in preparation, an athlete questions their ability to be great. Without confidence in a goal, an athlete feels unworthy. Without belief in a skill set, self-doubt destroys performance.

(Preparation + Realized Goals + Maximized Skill Set) x Confidence = Excellent Taper!

Chapter 8: Assistant Coaches

Sourcing and hiring exceptional coaches is intrinsic to the operation of a well-run team. The process isn't a perfect science. Many times, the best coach for your program is a passive candidate. Thus, you'll have to pursue them.

Identify the premier assistant coaches on the deck. I'm perpetually evaluating the programs and competitors in our marketplace. Look for quick spikes in success, performance, parent satisfaction, registration, and retention. I have this inherent desire to know why other teams and coaches are successful. If you keep your ear in conversations around the deck, you will find a good coach.

If you don't find a coach on deck, you'll have to source one through a job post. The job post provides a brief summary of your team's success, philosophy, and overall mission. Include your mission statement if you have one. I post specific expectations for our coaches. This eliminates those who need not apply. Certifications are mandatory to stay compliant with USA Swimming. However, if you're hiring a first-time coach, have a procedure in place to usher them through the certification process.

Responsibilities and coaching expectations are an integral part of a standard job posting. Responsibilities change from season to season, but the expectations give shape to the position. Expectations model strong leadership and are reviewed in the first interview.

List a salary range for each position you post. When I was in my twenties, the state of South Carolina called my name. I researched jobs and found a team with a vacancy. The club, a nonprofit organization with over 100 athletes, needed a senior-level coach. Even though I loved South Carolina, the compensation package had to make sense. The phone interview with the board of directors flowed well and lasted nearly an hour. The board president allowed time for questions, which I took full advantage of. Salary was at the top of my mind. I learned I'd take a tremendous pay cut to move to South Carolina (not to mention the cost of living is higher than in Cincinnati). I withdrew my name from the pool of candidates.

The best coach for your program may be an out-of-towner. Befriend talented coaches at travel meets and continue to grow your network. Prospect for future talent at coaches' conventions. Young coaches make multiple stops before settling in with their "forever job."

I hire coaches with high school swimming experience. Coaches engage significantly better when they've participated in the life cycle (age group through senior) of the sport. Hire for character and teach skills. Coaches improve with time, experience, and failure. I've developed a coaching style through mentorship. Experience and shadowing coaches (without directly poaching their style) paved the way for me to evolve and become an effective coach. Unfortunately, some coaches hide their tricks of the trade from their assistant coaches. Great coaches and mentors share best practices, even if it means they give up their proprietary information. Books and certifications can't replace direct education from a more experienced coach.

I look for nine qualities in an assistant swim coach. If all qualified interviewees possess these seven traits, I have a tie breaker.

Aaron's Nine Traits for Success

1. A good person with an open heart to love and learn
2. Emotional connection to swimming
3. Grit and the ability to problem solve
4. Ambition
5. Responsibility
6. Enthusiasm
7. No fear of failure

8. Agility
9. Punctuality

If I have a decision to make between two or more candidates, I ask myself one question: What can I learn from this coach? New coaches add value through experience and perspective.

When reaching out to potential candidates, prepare them for the process. I have four conversations with each candidate. If the person is from my personal network, I'll omit a conversation or two. The first interaction is a "soft touch" through email. I'll thank them for applying, exchange pleasantries, and set up the next touch: a brief phone call of thirty minutes. This call gives them the opportunity to learn more about our program. I'll also gather information: What is their coaching philosophy? Why did they choose coaching as a career or part-time job? What is their biggest success and failure? What type of leadership do they thrive under (often a smoke-out question)?

If the phone call inspires you, request a personal interview. If the applicant arrives late or dressed inappropriately for an interview, the conversation is short. I won't waste my time.

I start the interview with a brief overview of our program. I'll summarize recent successes, opportunities to grow, areas for improvement, culture, and philosophy. The questions I ask are situational and thought-provoking.

- If a team parent is speaking poorly about your program in public, how would you handle it?
- Have you had negative interactions with a coach or team you've worked for? If so, how did you address it?
- After learning more about our program, how will you add tremendous value to our coaching staff/team?

- If you walked into a dinner party, would you feel more comfortable with the host introducing you or would you initiate conversations with guests on your own?
- If you host a dinner party, are you more frustrated with those who show up fifteen minutes early or fifteen minutes late? Why?
- What do you enjoy most about coaching?
- Do you see yourself as a head coach within the next three to five years?

Keep the interview to an hour.

The next step is to evaluate the coach in action. I'll have the candidate run an age-appropriate or group-specific workout. If the coach does these three things, they're hired.

1. The first is the clear expression of process. Evaluate their ability to relay training sets and provide technical instruction.

2. Second, they must objectively qualify engagement from both the coach and athletes. Enthusiastic coaches capture the attention of athletes. I hire fun coaches!

3. The third thing I look for is command. Athletes respond and respect coaches with presence.

If everything works out, the coach is a fit. Draft an offer letter reviewing specific expectations and responsibilities for the position. Assistant coaches drive your program, so make sure you surround yourself with the best people in the business.

Chapter 9: Coaching Your Coaches

Head coaches with above-average leadership acumen develop their staff through training and support. Assistant coaches are the face of the brand and represent the organization both in and out of the pool. Coaches evolve from their experiences and learn from personal mistakes and objections. Teachable moments transform coaches.

I've hired incredible assistant coaches in my career. These associates leaned on me for leadership and time. The most important resource you can provide an assistant coach is time. Assistants are your biggest advocates, cheerleaders, and supporters. Reciprocate this admiration with your time. Share your experiences. Be a sounding board. Offer time for questions, time to vent frustrations, time to talk technique, and, most importantly, time to be creative.

Years ago, I hired an amazing coach named Dave. He dropped by my office on a regular basis and provided updates on his group. Dave walked me through each set for his 11-and 12-year-olds and *demanded* feedback. He went the extra mile to care and connect with me. Those conversations not only made Dave a better coach, but they elevated us to one of the top brands in Ohio.

Detail-oriented head coaches exercise a term I call engaged corrective analysis (ECA). ECA is a simple way of processing a peripheral conversation, either visually or audibly, and developing a resolution as necessary. Create an actionable, corrective methodology for issues within your program. Have you overheard a technical conversation between a coach and athlete but the information shared was incorrect? Here's an example illustrating ECA.

"When you swim butterfly, drive your thumbs down in the water first. Keep your chin low the entire time. Then, pull the hands wide outside of the shoulders before accelerating the hands to the hips."

How would you redirect your coach with incorrect stroke instruction like this? Here's what I'd say: "I like your emphasis on head position when teaching butterfly. Head position is an important concept to review before each training set."

Next, provide support through ECA: "Even though sculling out wide provides leverage and potential power for the swimmer, it also creates inefficiencies in the stroke cycle. I've had success by teaching a flat-hand entry on fly and accelerating the hands directly toward the hips."

ECA captures conversations and demonstrations necessary for coach development.

Treating a coach to lunch or rewarding an assistant in front of his or her peers is a first-class move. Be genuine and authentic by making the experience about your assistant coach.

Scrimmaging is the most underutilized skill a coach has in his or her tool belt. Train side-by-side with your staff to be better every day. Scrimmaging and role-playing are methods to prepare for any scenario on deck.

Assistant coaches yearn for more information on kinesiology, physiology, and anatomy. Organize learning opportunities in these areas of study. Allow your coaches to grow through clinics and swim camps.

Prepare your coaches for the next chapter in their career. To do this, you must supervise them appropriately.

Chapter 10: Supervising Your Coaches

A progressive head coach allows coaches to be creative and group managers. Don't micromanage your associates. Trust your coaches and continue to practice ECA.

I hired an incredible person to lead our 11- and 12-year-old group back in 2004. She was shy but uniquely enthusiastic when her athletes swam well. Her skillful touch as a stroke technician was special. At the conclusion of one practice, I paid her a compliment: "I overheard your conversation with David about his breaststroke kick. He was engaged the entire time and I'm sure he appreciated it. Nice job!"

She grinned and said, "I told the kids when Coach Aaron is around, we have to be really good and listen. If not, I might not be here tomorrow and he'll be the one coaching you. They think you're mean and scary since you coach the older athletes."

I laughed so hard I cried.

Chapter 11: Moving on from Coaches

Coaches are held to a high standard in our society, much like schoolteachers and religious leaders. We are watched, studied, and critiqued every minute of the day by swim families. If a coach is publicly or privately out of line, it can cripple an organization. Coaches work with impressionable people and thus need to model appropriate behaviors.

Corrective action from the head coach or board normally follows egregious behavior. If a situation threatens the safety of club members or the reputation of the team, termination is the only choice. Firing an associate is emotional, stressful, and downright uncomfortable. I've let two coaches go. In both cases, I lost friends and multiple nights of sleep.

Every team or club has a detailed code of conduct for their staff. Since my most recent employer was part of a health-delivery system, their code of conduct took precedence. First-class programs have associate handbooks. Your assistant coaches are required to read the handbook and code of conduct before they step on deck. Create a signoff page for certification and affiliation to these rules and regulations.

I won't highlight every situation that requires immediate termination. Anything in question will be directed toward USA Swimming. When the rubber meets the road, ask this question: Does the egregious act from your coach put athletes at risk or violate state/national laws, rules, and responsibilities within the framework of your team?

Minor infractions are part of the business, especially with part-time and seasonal employees. Tardiness, poor customer service, and dress code violations deserve another opportunity. Insubordination, acts of indecency (sexual or otherwise), failure to carry out critical tasks, public intoxication, sexual misconduct, inappropriate communication, and social media outbursts carry heavy consequences. Coaches are suspended, dismissed, placed on leave, and, with significant cause, terminated. Provide specific and detailed information to your local law enforcement as necessary.

***

Termination requires patience and an open mind. First, gather information from all parties involved in the incident. Take detailed notes and ask as many open-ended questions as possible. Maintain a non-adversarial body position throughout your interviews and don't verbalize opinions or judgments. From time to time, someone may ask for anonymity. Please comply with their request (unless the information is illegal and needs to be passed on to law enforcement).

Next, make an informed decision based on the collected information. Objective data is vital in the process (texts, emails, photographs, etc.). Schedule a face-to-face meeting with the associate (again, after the initial interviews once you've made your informed decision). Get to the point right away. If you're firing the coach, avoid small talk. The process is specific, truth-driven, and actionable. Don't apologize for the unfortunate circumstances. Keep the meeting to ten minutes unless the coach has questions. He or she may form a rebuttal, in which case you should circle back around to your decision. If you change your decision, you're to blame. You should have asked more questions. Don't get emotional during the conversation.

Here's a sample termination for a case in which a coach uses colorful language to describe his thoughts on a new practice schedule. He doesn't do anything illegal or against the law. However, he doesn't model appropriate cultural expectations for the club.

"Thank you for meeting with me today, coach Bunny Rabbit. I'm here to inform you that we're letting you go. I took a few days to process the meetings with our swim families as well as our conversation on Monday. The screenshots of vulgar language through email and text are not only inappropriate but undercut the culture of our entire organization. I've determined we have to move forward in a positive direction. I need you to surrender all club possessions and belongings immediately. I'll mail you your final check. You'll no longer be able to reach out to our coaches and athletes to discuss this incident. I'll walk you to the front door."

Chapter 12: The Moment of Truth for Athletes

The moment of truth for an athlete is the candid result of grit, attitude, behavior, and training. Success is intentional and many times, failure is too. Nothing is more important than grit. If you were backed into a corner, would you fight yourself out of it without grit? Grit doesn't quit.

Results-driven activity is fueled by attitude. Attitude determines altitude. In swimming, we generate objective results from this one trait. Attitude is asking yourself: "Will I do everything in my power to improve today, or will I go through the motions?" Many would call this character. I call it attitude. Attitude controls training, performance, and everything in between.

The moment of truth is a harsh reality check. How many times have you told an athlete to stop pulling on the lane line? What about the swimmer who skips warm-ups because he needs to adjust his goggles forty-seven times? And, have you had an athlete who refuses to move over to a more challenging interval because he or she isn't feeling it today? When it comes to being great, attitude is the low-hanging fruit. This is the easiest thing to improve. Great athletes with positive attitudes never have a ceiling for greatness. They're always sitting in a convertible.

Behavior molds greatness. Practice behavior is an essential part of the moment of truth. If an athlete trains poorly, they'll swim poorly at the championship meet. One of my top athletes ten years ago had horrendous practice behaviors. She gave up on test sets, lacked discipline in the weight room, and was a terrible listener (she wouldn't change her technique if you asked politely). Two weeks before the championship meet, I pulled out a note card. On it, I predicted her time for each event I entered her in. On the bottom of the card, I jotted: "Someone can't expect to swim fast with poor practice behavior."

The meet ended and I overheard a conversation she was having with one of her teammates. "I'm not sure why Aaron isn't giving me high fives and telling me I did a good job. I'm not happy with how I swam but I still did okay."

I was right on with my time predictions. The world works one way and one way only. Success is a cumulative effort of discipline, focus, dedication, determination, hustle, and education. These are the essential characteristics that fall under behavior. Life will not give you a high five when you don't deserve it. Behaviors turn into habits. Habits control the outcome.

Training is the guts of the moment of truth. The late swimmers in the water are always late. The lazy swimmers push off the bottom of the pool and pull on the lane line. The hard workers lead the lanes and stay after practice to stretch. One of my former athletes, a sophomore in high school at the time, came to me with a list of goals. I reviewed the list with him and one stood out more than the others. He wanted to complete twenty pull-ups and twenty push-ups in one minute by the end of his senior year. Now, I'm a fit guy (okay, I *was* a fit guy), but forty reps of anything related to body weight in a minute is tough to do. I asked him what his action plan was. This is what he did: He arrived every day to our fitness center ten minutes before practice and went through the one-minute routine. He started with pull-ups each time. By the end of his junior year, he muscled up twenty pull-ups and fourteen push-ups. Midway through his senior year, he hit his goal.

Elated, he clapped my back with his sweaty hand. With a big, banana grin, he said, "Coach, I did it!"

I smiled back and said, "I'm proud of you. You accomplished your goal!"

I'll never forget what he said next.

"Coach, I can do better. I'm shooting for twenty-five of each now. I feel the pain now, but I'll feel the strength down the road."

His training aligned with his goals. Be intentional. Be great.

Chapter 13: College Swimming

Our goal as coaches and mentors is to prepare our athletes for the challenges and rigors of college. Coaches usher swim families through the process of finding the academic and athletic fit for their children. I set up a conference with the swimmer, along with his or her guardians, to discuss the proper fit for athletics.

Before we meet, ask the athlete to complete a simple homework assignment. The athlete must create a list of their top ten schools and state why each institution is unique. Meet with your athlete and his or her parents after the homework assignment. The goal of the conversation is to rank the academic, athletic, and even social must-haves. The following is an excerpt from one of my athletes.

Academic

1. A highly respected business school

2. A school that shows successful placement of students in jobs after graduation

3. Challenging curriculum

4. Allows me to co-op or shadow with companies/businesses

5. I'd like to be within four hours of home.

Athletic

1. A coach who makes me a well-rounded swimmer (and a faster one)

2. A coach who focuses on the team goals versus individual performances

3. A nice and new pool

4. A program that finishes first or second in their conference year after year; I am looking at Division II or III

5. Tutors and a student-athlete learning center

<u>Social</u>

1. I'd love to have a good basketball or football team to root for.

2. Be in an area that has outdoor activities close by such as skiing

3. Low crime area

4. Allows me to have a car on campus

5. I'd like to walk to shops and a grocery store if I need to pick something up.

These three lists perpetuate a discussion, as does financial assistance. Money determines the best fit for a student-athlete unless a scholarship covers the cost of college. A stat sheet, which includes test scores, GPA, and general metrics, serves as an agenda. Feel free to ask questions related to swimming. Which options fit their skill set in the pool? Would they score at conference? Is the swim team fully funded? Do men and women train together?

I conclude the conversation with one final point. Club coaches talk to colleges about an athlete's character, personality, accountability, and discipline. Promoting my athlete to a college program is like selling a used car. If you sell a car, be transparent. Disclose the oil leaks, body damage, alignment issues, and accidents. You may "forget" to mention the radio dial sticks in hot weather and the middle seat belt is broken.

College coaches rely on us to be honest and share our experiences. What do we discuss?

- Personality and demeanor
- Practice attendance, motivation, and effort
- Progress and improvement through your program
- The relationship with parents, as college coaches communicate with parents on a regular basis

If you gain medical consent from the athlete and family, you can talk about injuries. Injuries with the shoulder, knee, hip, back, or ankle impact performance and time in the pool. Significant concerns such as diabetes, syncope, history of seizures, and hypertension are discussed privately by the family and athlete during the recruiting process.

Years ago, I coached an amazing athlete talented enough to score at most Division I conference meets. Four or five colleges reached out to me regularly in hopes of signing her. I offered each coach the opportunity to discuss her character with me. They all immediately brought up her Facebook account.

"Greta" (not her name but I want to protect her identity) displayed several pictures of herself at parties with college-age boys. One photo showed her on a boat with beer and a pack of cigarettes. Though the pictures weren't vulgar or indecent, it did raise concern. College athletes are the face of their institutions. Thus, they have a responsibility to represent the brand well. A school eventually took a chance on her, but unfortunately, she failed out of school within the first semester.

The purpose of a meeting with a college coach is a simple. Start the process. Ask your athletes to fill out the online questionnaires for each school that meets their interest. Questionnaires take about twenty to twenty-five minutes to complete. Direct them to highlight test scores, GPA, volunteer activities, school clubs, honors, leadership ability, awards, and athletic performance. Coach them to follow up with the schools they reach out to. Let them know it's their responsibility (not yours) to send brief emails to the head swim coach from time to time with updated times, goals, and competitions your team is preparing for.

Club coaches working with senior-level athletes know the procedures and rules regarding contact, phone calls, texts, emails, and personal visits with college programs. Review these policies with your families and athletes. Rules change from year to year, so educate yourself on the newest and latest in college recruiting. I recommend allowing a college coach or two each year to visit with your athletes about the recruiting process. Most do it without pitching their own program.

Chapter 14: Bullying

USA Swimming is doing their part to end bullying. I'm confident we'll save lives because of their commitment to end this terrible and destructive behavior. Coaches need to be vigilant in handling these incidents immediately. Before the USA Swimming policy was updated, we approached bullying directly.

A few years ago, a Twitter war erupted between two of my athletes. It began as playful banter. Then, one of the swimmers made a derogatory statement about the other boy's girlfriend. I heard everything the next day after practice. Fortunately, both boys were at dryland. I brought the boys into my office but interviewed them separately. I gathered every bit of information I could, including the Twitter screenshots.

Both had their side of the story. Through active listening, I was able to uncover the details. Each was at fault. Fortunately, they owned their fair share of guilt and apologized to one another. I spoke to both sets of parents and stated I'd suspend their sons if the social media war continued. Parental involvement needs to improve for us to halt bullying.

Assess harm within the scope of your practice. Children in danger of physical, mental, or emotional harm need assistance from a professional resource. Handle these cases with extreme sensitivity and confidentiality.

Between my freshman and sophomore year in college, I helped coach a small summer swim club. I assisted the lead coach with stroke instruction and meet coverage. In our group, we had a large 12-year-old boy who was approximately thirty to fifty pounds heavier than his peers. I thought he was 15 or 16 years old! One of our assistants called him the "big nasty monster" because of his height and weight. Halfway through the season, his mother asked me for a few minutes of my time and I obliged. I could tell something was bothering her.

"My son's only wish is to look like everyone else in his age group. He has struggled with body image his entire life. I'm embarrassed to talk to his coach about it because I don't want to hurt his feelings at all. However, I wanted you to know so you could keep an eye on him."

I was heartbroken over his mother's pleas. The following week, her son quit the team. As a staff, we issued an apology to the boy and family. Days after the apology, several members of our board offered to pay for the services of a local sports psychologist, as well as a registered dietitian, to help the family out. Fortunately, he received help and eventually made it back to the pool. Diving was his calling. As a coach, know what you're saying and how you're saying it. If you see a child struggling, act with empathy and a warm heart.

Resolve bullying immediately. Head coaches set the standard for their program. The conversation with everyone is never fun. Conversations with the victim are kept confidential. Understand that re-integrating a bullied swimmer back into team activities can be a slow process. Have weekly huddles with the victim's family to monitor progress. Build confidence with every conversation and keep a close eye on their body language. Carefully analyze facial expressions, interactions with other athletes, and practice effort.

Address bullying before the first practice of the season. Tell your team that nothing is more important to the team than the health and safety of all swimmers.

Chapter 15: Dealing with Other Members of Your Pool

Normally, club swim teams train at pools owned and managed by another entity. Challenges surface when members at these pools compete for lanespace with your athletes. Prime times for health and wellness clubs are typically five to eight a.m. and four thirty to seven thirty p.m. Fee-based classes, such as swimming lessons or water aerobics, are held at prime time to capture more business.

When I started Sea Wolves, I had my share of confrontations. We had thirty-two athletes with varying skill levels in four lanes at prime time. Our pool, a six-lane 25-yard pool, was rarely utilized by lap swimmers of the health club. Yet, we had to leave two lanes open if someone wanted to swim or water walk. We simply couldn't get quality training in with the number of athletes in the pool.

One day, I'd had it up to my nose with crowded lanes. Our entire team of thirty-two athletes showed up on deck. I moved a few swimmers over to one of the open lap-swim lanes, which was against club policy, to free up space in the four lanes we trained in. Five minutes later, two lap swimmers arrived. Both appeared visibly upset with me. I calmly spoke to them about the situation. One of the ladies understood our dilemma. The other woman blew up on me. She grabbed her towel, changed into her clothes, and went upstairs to cancel her membership. Fortunately, she calmed down once she met our general manager (and he offered a free month of dues for the inconvenience). I called her after practice to apologize because I felt horrible. She appreciated the call.

In 2009, our team made tremendous strides and we grew to 200 members. Nearly 35 percent of our team qualified for USA Swimming Junior Olympic or National time standards. The team was in great shape, but unfortunately, our lane lines weren't. Chips and pieces of hard plastic were everywhere in and around the pool. I called a meeting with our new aquatics director to talk about the risks of having lane lines in this condition. We made the decision to scrap the old lines and purchase a new set for the club. One of our high-maintenance members voiced his displeasure with the decision.

Steve, a member of the club for over six years, believed fins and kickboards should be prioritized over lane lanes. We patiently listened to his argument and then shared our concerns. Broken lane lines with frayed wires are dangerous to all swimmers and lifeguards.

He snapped back at us. "You just don't get it! Lane lines are only important for the swim team!"

Lap swimmers use the lane lines. Swim lessons use the lane lines. *He* was using the lane lines. I apologized for the lack of usable fins and kickboards we had in stock. I ordered new equipment immediately after our meeting. Later in the month, he thanked me. He even told me he was out of line for his tone.

I have many stories, but this one takes the cake. Over the holiday break, we move our main practices to the morning. The schedule change caused a major disruption in the regular lap pool schedule. As a courtesy to our members, I posted an addendum with the short-term change addressed in large, bold letters. The communication occurred three weeks before holiday training. We left two lanes open for lap swimmers and I made sure the signs were posted everywhere.

On the first morning of holiday training, fifteen athletes jumped in the pool at seven o'clock. I started the athletes off with a swim and kick mix. Halfway through our warm-up, two women arrived on deck. Both looked puzzled and confused with the amount of swimmers in the pool. The women escorted the lifeguard on duty over to my side of the deck. I knew this was trouble.

"Your kids make too many waves. They kick too hard and they splashed us when we were trying to float. Your athletes are in the lanes we normally use." They awaited my reaction and response.

I stayed calm and kept my poise. My swimmers are members of the club and they pay to cover program dues. Fee-based programs help drive membership costs down. Nonetheless, they had two empty lanes open. Why were they upset? The signs were up, emails went out, and the website was updated.

"I do apologize for the inconvenience. We'll be in the pool for the next ten days at this time. You're more than welcome to use the pool before or after us. If you'd like, I can reserve your lanes with a cone."

The lifeguard made copies of the temporary schedule. Obviously, they were both sign-blind. So, why is this my favorite story? One of the women had a grandson in my group. She was supposed to pick him up and take him to practice, but she forgot about it!

***

Finding pool time and handling other members of the club is a challenge. What can you do to make everyone happy?

- Kill members with kindness and you'll create supportive fans. Begin each conversation with a smile and introduction, even if the situation is one you'd rather not be in.
- The customer isn't always right, but they're a valued customer. Empathize with their needs and address the concerns with kindness.
- Listen first. Speak second. Customers and members of the facility want to vent to someone (even when the problem isn't your fault).Be an active listener and resist becoming adversarial.
- Be engaged during the conversation and offer solutions. If a member doesn't see a posted schedule change, ask them how they'd like to

receive the information. He or she may prefer an email over signage. Capture their information and offer to communicate directly with them.

- After a conversation, ask the member if you've successfully answered their questions and addressed their concerns.
- If possible, address the customer or member by their name throughout the conversation.
- If you need to involve a supervisor, manager on duty, or other associate in conversation, proceed without completely abandoning the customer. For example, if a member complains about the lap pool being too cold, don't run off for twenty minutes looking for the aquatics manager. Kindly ask the member to have a seat in the aquatics office while you text or page the aquatics manager. If the manager doesn't get back to you in a timely manner (in three to five minutes), have the member provide their availability to continue the conversation at a later date.
- Recognize we're not perfect. Arguments regarding pool time, schedules, loud athletes, and equipment typically last longer than they should because neither party wants to be wrong. Let your guard down and absorb the blow. In the long run, you'll gain a raving fan.

Chapter 16: Fundraising and Support

Programming dues are the lifeblood of club swim teams, while additional financial support through fundraising transforms clubs from good to great. Often, these opportunities are neglected because our basic club needs are being met. What about the big-ticket items? Which tools separate your club from the pack? Many for-profit organizations term these purchases as capital projects. Larger purchases, such as power towers, buckets, backstroke ledges, and underwater cameras, are impressive. Think impressive and take massive action! As a forward-thinking coach, I urge you to budget in big-ticket items on your wish list.

With the standard nonprofit structure, club teams have a board member responsible for fundraising. The head coach communicates with this parent on a regular basis to come up with the most viable opportunities for fundraising. What are you fundraising for? What are your needs?

Make the financial commitment to retain your coaches. One of the best assistants I shared the deck with was a full-time teacher. He made about $35,000 a year. We should've found a way to match his annual income through fundraisers and make him a salaried coach. He left our club to become a full-time coach. Great teams need gifted coaches on deck. Make coaching a priority over gadgets.

***

Invest in team outings and trips with your club. Improve retention and avoid attrition by adding dynamic and engaging activities to the schedule. Educational team outings inspire and create opportunities for growth. Would you set up a training trip to the Olympic Training Center in Colorado Springs for those who qualified for Nationals? The team may not be able to cover the entire expense. However, if you partnered with another team, you could defray the cost of the trip. It's an excellent opportunity for you to learn best practices from another coach and provide an unparalleled experience for your athletes. Could you take your athletes to a Duel in the Pool meet? It would inspire your younger athletes. Could you organize a formal dinner with a guest speaker (Olympian, top-tier coach, etc.), dancing, and awards? Our club team did this and the athletes loved the experience. Activities such as these produce a buzz in the community and with your team.

Swim programs never get enough pool time. Coaches specialize training with less interruption when there's more space to work with. Use your resources for pool rental. If your team trains under a roof year-round, get them outside in the summer.

The community is charitable. People donate to organizations that create opportunities for young athletes. Here are some ideas your athletes can implement to create massive action.

- Sell gift cards. Hundreds of teams go this route and bring in thousands of dollars each season.
- Work local events in exchange for donations to your club team.
- Host a car wash and sell baked goods, lemonade, and bottled drinks. A team in our area did this and his organization received $1,000 in four hours!
- Host a silent auction. Ask for donations (such as autographed sports memorabilia and art) from your families and the community. Donations are tax write-offs.
- Swimming laps for cash (USA Swimming has their own branded program) is a slam dunk. To make it more special, have your swim parents take part by doing it with their children.
- Sell team-branded spirit wear through an outside vendor. These companies kick back a percentage of sales to the team. We once sold approximately $12,000 worth of items and it netted us $1,800.

- Partner with a restaurant and have them dedicate a portion of sales to your team. The last restaurant we worked with gave us 10 percent of their net sales on Wednesday nights between six and seven p.m. because we sent our families over after practice. We increased their customer load and they incentivized us.
- Promote businesses, sponsors, and partners on your team shirts, banners, and website. One coach told me his club received $2,500 *every month* from five companies. This revenue alone supports a full-time assistant coach.
- Add a donation line or contribution check box to your registration paperwork. Asking for the gift early in the season is better than asking at the end. Provide donation values of $10, $25, $50, $100, and other. If every family on our team gifted $10, we'd have an additional $2,650 to work with.

Send frequent updates to your stakeholders and families on how the team will use raised funds. Motivate your swim families to give each season.

Chapter 17: Health of a Coach

Creating an elite swim team requires accountability, responsibility, time, and discipline. The pressure and stress that comes along with managing a team will wear down the best coaches in the world. At age 26, I started a swim team from scratch. The infrastructure wasn't there as it is with many teams. Our team was a true start-up.

I was youthful and full of passion. My vision was to create something that would challenge the balance of local swimming. The community recognized our desire to become a local and regional powerhouse. And it all started from my vision.

I took full advantage of being young, single, and fit. Before meets and after practices, I'd exercise for an hour. I ate healthier than anyone I knew. Life was easy.

Eventually, my work responsibilities increased. I received a promotion without a raise. Management added payroll, meetings, and annual reviews to my plate. I worried about everything. Stress, paranoia, and insomnia paralyzed me before I ever stepped foot in my office for the day. Fast food and laziness replaced salads and exercise.

In 2015, I ballooned up to 237 pounds, which was my highest weight by 17 pounds. Sarah noticed the waist of my favorite slacks were under incredible duress. I'm glad she was polite about it. I scheduled an annual wellness exam for insurance purposes. The exam measured weight, body mass index (BMI), blood pressure, and resting heart rate. Labs were drawn, so I fasted the previous day.

I arrived at the doctor's office full of confidence despite my appearance. After a brief time in the waiting room, the nurse called me back to the exam room. She quickly ushered me up to the scale. In bright red numbers, it read "237.4." The nurse sheepishly whispered to me.

"Mr. Dorfman, are you intentionally trying to gain weight?"

Her comment crushed my feelings. Two years ago, I had weighed 200 pounds.

It shook me up. The cold exam room didn't help either. All I could do was sit and play on my phone while the muted conversations went on in the hallway. Minutes later, a different nurse came in to check my blood pressure. She attached a Velcro cuff around my arm and pumped it until it made a small hiss. The reading was high.

"Sir, you need to calm down. I have 140 over 90, which is pre-hypertensive. Perhaps you're just a little nervous."

I was more than nervous. The first five minutes of my visit seemed like a death march.

Two days after my appointment, I received a phone call. The results from my blood test presented hyperlipidemia (elevated cholesterol). One year of poor nutrition, stress, and inactivity had brought this on. I needed to get healthy.

The Moment of Truth for Coaches

Being a swim coach is more than tending to the needs of athletes. Top coaches model healthy behaviors. When the nurse weighed me, I had a moment of truth.

Embrace each moment of truth and evolve.

Coaches struggle with health. I've talked to several colleagues who want to eat better or exercise, only to find out weeks later they've given up. Expect to encounter challenges and be actionable every day.

Nutrition

As a registered dietitian, I understand the value of a nutritious diet. Unfortunately, swim meets aren't the best place to find healthy selections.

I traveled to Winter Juniors in Knoxville, Tennessee, about eight years ago. Our team entered one athlete in four events for the week. Since the gaps between her races were huge, I naturally did what all coaches do. I retreated to the hospitality area to play on my laptop and eat.

When I walked into the room (it was under a large circus tent), I noticed a group of coaches huddled around a large chocolate fountain. Near the fountain were cookies, pre-cut cake slices, and pudding. It didn't take long for me to partake in the feeding frenzy. After all, my sweet tooth is very sensitive. Temi (my athlete) visited the tent before her 100 freestyle. She asked me two questions. Question one: "What should I do for warm-up?"

Question number two was about my appearance. "What's all over your mouth? Is it chocolate pudding?"

Guilty as charged.

Weight management is 80 percent nutrition and 20 percent physical activity. We can't outrun, outswim, or out-lift a poor diet. Poor diets lead to comorbidities. Comorbidities lead to bigger problems down the road.

The first step in reforming a poor diet is maintaining a diary. Log the foods you eat and include meal times, the preparation method, and portion sizes. Review your diary at the end of each week by tracking food with a spreadsheet or an app. If you're using a spreadsheet, separate food groups into categories such as fruits, vegetables, starches, proteins, dairy, fats, and sugars. When you review your diet diary, what catches your eye the most? Are you binging at night? Do you eat breakfast every day? Are you dining out more than you should?

The second step is educating yourself on proper nutrition. Books, websites, and blogs authored by registered dietitians are the only resources I recommend. An important part of this step is scheduling an appointment with a registered dietitian. Registered dietitians are credentialed clinicians in nutrition science. Dietitians specialize their focus, much like doctors. When you meet with a dietitian, request a basic meal plan with substitute foods and a healthy grocery list to shop with. Energy needs are important as well. For a dietitian to calculate your energy needs, he or she needs information on your medical history, height, weight, daily physical activity, food preferences, and medications. Follow-up appointments, either weekly or monthly, are important if adjustments with the plan are necessary.

The third step with your nutrition plan is locating an accountability tool. Log your nutritional intake with an app or simply place a whiteboard in your kitchen with healthy reminders.

The fourth step is to get someone, such as a colleague or spouse, to sponsor your healthy endeavor. "Diet" is a word I never use. "Eating nutritionally sound" is more appropriate. Support is the best way to sponsor a friend. Hopefully, your sponsor tries healthy foods with you or matches your intake of vegetables each day.

After step four, develop a strategy with a set of short-term objectives and goals. Start with a list of three or four strategies and then add to it once those objectives become a habit. Here are some strategies to consider.

- Eat smaller, more frequent meals every four to five hours. Research shows consuming smaller, more frequent meals elevates resting metabolic rate and in turn burns more calories at rest. If your digestive system is constantly running, satiety improves.
- People with more body water have more lean body mass. Muscle is metabolically active tissue. Drink water!

- Mix your macronutrients. Carbohydrates, proteins, and fats are the three macronutrients. There are both good and bad choices in each macronutrient group. When combined, macronutrients elevate your metabolism.
- Dine out with a healthy mindset. Order salads over large entrées, drink water instead of carbonated beverages, and choose lunch portions if offered. Ask for sauce and dressing on the side. Replace starches with vegetables.
- Alcohol sabotages metabolism, so avoid consuming more than four drinks per week. Alcohol elevates blood pressure, spikes blood triglycerides (fats), increases insulin resistance, and stores excess calories as adipose tissue.
- Try a plant-based diet. Vegetables, fruits, beans, nuts, seeds, and hearty grains are delicious. Set a goal to try one new fruit or vegetable every month.
- Avoid a fat-free diet. Increase your intake of the monounsaturated and polyunsaturated fats found in flax, chia, fish, avocado, olives, nuts, seeds, and plant-based oils.
- Taper your carbohydrates through the day. Consume more carbohydrates when your body is up and running.
- Fiber is important. A healthy diet contains 25 to 30 grams per day. Fresh fruits, beans, vegetables, whole grains, and nuts are good sources of fiber.

Physical Activity

An exercise routine improves productivity and energy levels. The subtle balance of resistance training and cardiovascular exercise is recommended for weight management and strength building.

Personal trainers plan around the physical activities you enjoy. Hiking is my favorite pastime when I'm not working. A personal trainer can create an exercise prescription starting with this information.

Trainers develop a plan backed by science, experience, and common sense. After all, a good plan is safe, appropriate, and adaptable. The common coach-ism is "No pain, no gain." After a certain age, pain leads to injury. Injury leads to setbacks. And setbacks last weeks, months, or even years. Identify exercises specific to your goals. Exercise plans are adaptable. Develop a program for your home, the hotel, and the pool.

Accountability and discipline are essentials with a successful exercise program. Encourage a colleague or friend within your network to walk with you. Track your workouts. Find a way to make it work consistently.

Stress and Sleep

Highly motivated, goal-oriented coaches hold themselves to a high standard. Developing elite athletes and coaches challenges the best leaders in the business. With these expectations, the amount of stress a coach goes through can be unbearable.

The coaching fraternity in the Greater Cincinnati area is very close. I have a monthly standing lunch meeting with a colleague I've known for thirty years. We talk shop and use one another as a sounding board. The time is spent in reflection. We share best practices, offer transparent feedback, and even deliver tough love. No matter what we discuss, I always feel better after lunch. Use your colleagues as a sounding board. Lean on close friends, particularly fellow coaches, when times get stressful.

Stress, if ignored, is toxic. Years ago, we had a nice family on our team with two boys five years apart in age. The parents struggled to make ends meet, but they desperately wanted to have their children in the pool. Since they couldn't afford to pay the fees in two transactions (per our billing process), I offered to create a separate plan. The family made monthly payments when Dad received his bonus check from work. It was a nightmare keeping track of everything.

Midway through the season, the payments ceased. I received a short email from their mother with an explanation. It simply said, "We need money for vacation and food. I can't pay our dues this month." Immediately, I picked up the phone and called her. She didn't answer, so I left a voicemail.

I heard nothing from her for two weeks, though she continued to drop her sons off at practice without payment. She avoided me. I left numerous voicemails on her cell and home phone. I'm sure she received them. The boys had no idea what was going on and I wasn't going to involve them. We kept them in the pool. I went home every night stressed about it, and the situation created insomnia.

The situation worsened. My supervisor pulled the unpaid report and saw one of our families with an unsettled balance. The team was down $500 and I was on the hook for it. I made it a point to be in the front of the building at drop-off the next day. I waited for her in the rotunda. At ten till four, their van pulled up to the sidewalk. Immediately, our eyes locked. I could tell she was ready to pull off. Calmly, I walked over and greeted her.

"Hi. I hope you're doing well. Have you been receiving my calls? I'd sure like to talk about swim team registration."

Her face was blank and expressionless. Then, after a minute, she spoke. "I'm really embarrassed we took advantage of you. I'll have the check tomorrow. I promise. Please let the boys swim today."

I obliged her request. However, we never received the check. I finally came clean to my supervisor and told her I struck a separate payment plan with this family to keep the kids on the team. I was able to track their mom down later in the week at drop-off. She apologized again. Unfortunately, she couldn't pay the bill, and they left our team.

Her behavior left me stressed out. However, losing her family wasn't the end of the world. With every stressful situation, ask yourself one question: Will it matter in five years? If the answer is no, you can let it go. Control what can be controlled.

Stress makes us better or disrupts our lives. "Positive" stress is eustress. Coaches and swimmers thrive on eustress throughout the championship season. Eustress is euphoric anxiety blended with positive energy. The most recent championship meet we went to was full of eustress. The crowd was loud. Swimmers had tremendous time drops. National age-group records were set. Pool records were smashed. The announcer was engaged and enthusiastic. The feel of the meet reminded me of a professional football game. I had goosebumps, butterflies in my stomach, and anxiety all in one. With so much stimulation, I was engaged. If I wasn't having fun, there would've been something wrong with me. Coaches thrive in this environment. We coach for these moments. I didn't sleep much that trip. I couldn't wait to do everything again the next day.

Distress is the negative and detrimental form of stress. Distress comes in two forms: external and internal. Environmental factors and events that cause emotional harm create external distress. Self-manufactured thoughts that wreak havoc on your mind and body form internal distress. I suffered from internal distress as a competitive swimmer because I dwelled on bad swims and overthought the taper process. I simply couldn't overcome it.

Sleep is important because it's one of the few pauses we get for recovery. Emphasize the quality of sleep you need. Eat bananas and avocados before bed to relax. Bananas contain magnesium and potassium, which are natural muscle relaxants. Both bananas and avocados elevate melatonin levels (a hormone that controls sleep cycles). Black out everything in your room to void stimulation. Eliminate light from alarm clocks, cable boxes, and phones to create a more relaxing environment. Stretch before bed and roll out with a foam roller. Doing this relieves tension in muscle tissue and improves circulation. The better you sleep, the better you coach.

Even with the appropriate amount of sleep, coaches get overwhelmed and burned out. In severe cases, it evolves into depression. Please alert your loved ones and trustworthy colleagues if you need help. Depression is more common in the coaching world than it is in the general population. These symptoms and feelings need to be addressed by a professional and managed with appropriate care.

Balancing Your Home and Social Life

I struggle with work-life balance. There is nothing more important to me than my wife, kids, family, and friends. Life wouldn't be worth living without them. We spend a tremendous amount of time on the pool deck. And, we have to be the best spouse, significant other, parent, or friend we can be. Nutrition, exercise and sleep aren't enough to regenerate our minds and bodies. We need to disconnect from our career every once in a while.

Coaches make a tremendous impact on athletes. Our swimmers model the behaviors we teach them. Swimming isn't everything. Teach them about life beyond the pool deck. Show them how important it is to spend time with family. Model behaviors of an engaged parent. Here are some ideas on how to disconnect from coaching.

- Take a long weekend with the family. You may miss a practice or two, but you hired confident assistants. Allow your coaches to write the workouts while you're out.
- Have a standing exercise date with someone each day. Schedule a racquetball match with a colleague, hire a personal trainer for a

lunchtime workout, swim with one of your assistants, or simply hit the trails with your headphones on.

- Surprise your kids by picking them up from school and taking them to dinner. Do this once a month.
- Every summer, have a weekend with your friends at the lake, even if it falls in the middle of the season.
- Go to work late on Mondays when you have a meet on weekends. In fact, just go in for practice.
- Take up a weekly hobby with your significant other.
- Set a date night with your significant other. You need this time together.
- Stop checking your email for more than an hour. Silence your phone for an afternoon.
- Hire someone to cut your grass and do other mundane chores around your house. Spend this time with your children instead.
- Schedule office hours for your athletes and swim parents. Set boundaries and avoid impromptu meetings unless they're absolutely necessary.
- The most important thing you can do when you're feeling overwhelmed is to use the word "no." Coaches feel obligated to make every meeting, attend all meet sessions, and work each practice. Swim coaches work seven days a week. Swim parents and supervisors may not understand, but we have to keep ourselves fresh, focused, and healthy to be effective coaches.

Chapter 18: The Parent Board

A healthy partnership between the head coach and parent board is essential for a successful swim team. Premier teams thrive when a coach works hand in hand with a board. All teams are operationally and essentially unique. The executive power and control for each coach is contingent on the team structure.

Successful board-managed teams understand the head coach is an expert when it comes to swimming-related decisions. These decisions include meet selection, team travel, team-hosted events, practice/meet policy, and athlete placement. Competent coaches earn the right to make these decisions without hesitation from the board. Address the decision-making process early in your tenure.

As head coach of a parent-board-managed team, what would you do in these situations?

1. The coach creates a practice attendance policy for the National Team secondary to dismal outcome at the midseason performance meet. The board doesn't see the need for a practice policy. One of the parent board members has a child in the National group and thinks a new policy will cause swimmers to leave the team. The board views the practice policy as a deterrent for potential athletes to join the team.
2. The coach wants to ban his 10-and-under athletes from competing in technical suits. The board's opinion is simple: Each parent has the right to buy the suit of their choice. The coach is condemned with parents saying, "It's not your place to make a decision for the family."
3. The coach thinks the team should split up their 13-and-over and 12-and-under athletes for a meet in July by sending the older swimmers to a prelim/final meet while the younger athletes go to a more relaxed

invitational. The board disapproves of this because several families have children competing in both meets.

The first example is commonplace with more competitive teams. Senior coaches set lofty team goals. To achieve them, athletes have to practice. The compromise would be separating the group. Create a group with dedicated senior swimmers and another one without requirements.

The second example is a challenge because of the financial component. Tech suits are expensive and not every family can afford them. USA Swimming established a policy for another reason: Tech suits hide fundamental flaws with body balance and technique, and, again, they're expensive. (Purchase a regular team suit one size smaller if they need to have the "tech like" feel). Besides, children grow out of them in a year.

Split meet weekends are common with larger teams. The level of competition outside your LSC, the format of the meet, and the time of year influence meet selection. Work with your board to do what's best for all swimmers from a competitive standpoint.

The parent board is essential for team management. Boards take care of the low-hanging fruit. For example, if you're preparing for Nationals, you have little time to deal with a registration or website issue. If you're managing summer club clinics, filling out purchase orders for pull buoys takes a backseat. If you need a morning off to recover from twenty-two straight days of work, the board will respond to a few phone calls and emails.

A good board works with the coach. An outstanding board works through the coach. The board projects the voice, vision, philosophy, and culture of the head coach. The standard swim team board consists of a president, vice president, secretary, treasurer, membership chair, competition chair, volunteer chair, special events coordinator, and site rep for each training base you have within your program. Top flight boards contribute quality perspectives and robust ideas. Everyone has a voice on the board, including you. Keep meetings brief, specific, and relevant. Develop short-term and long-term goals with your president. Be on the lookout for opportunities to advance and improve. These opportunities may include:

- Acquisitions or mergers with other teams in the area
- Sourcing star assistant coaches
- Setting up clinics at summer clubs to boost membership
- Fundraising opportunities to make capital purchases for pool and deck equipment
- Leasing additional pool space to start satellite programs
- Hosting meets and discussing the best format to lure more outside competition
- The best championship or travel meets to attend
- Exploring new staff positions(full time and part time)

Chapter 19: Swim Parents

A strong line of communication and feedback must exist between coaches and parents. Team parents support your vision, philosophy, culture, and management style. Without swim team parents, you don't have a program. Take care of their children. A former swim parent of mine once said the pool was her child's second home and I was the second father to her daughter. You won't receive a more touching compliment than that. I treat each athlete as if they are my own child.

The pool is undoubtedly their second home. On weekdays, my swimmers hit the pool at five fifteen a.m., head to school immediately after practice, come back to the pool after their last class, and train until seven fifteen p.m. Parents pick up their children at seven thirty, watch them devour dinner in five minutes and then send them to their rooms to study. Coaches get the special hours with children. By the time parents see their children after swim practice, the kids are incapable of holding a three-minute conversation without needing food or sleep. Parents depend on us to model appropriate behaviors, provide teachable moments, and encourage their children to reach unprecedented goals.

Successful programs ensure their parents, coaches, and athletes (the three partners) work seamlessly through every decision. The "triangle of success" among the partners allows situational compromise and transparent communication. I'll get into this partnership in a moment. The goal of the three partners is to harmoniously agree on training plans, cultural alignment, and discipline. When conflict or miscommunication within the "triangle of success" emerges, it causes disruption within the team.

Disruption is uncomfortable for all partners. Coaches have egos and take things personally. Parents love their children recklessly and seek control of their development. Athletes get caught in the middle of it all and aren't sure who to side with. When the rubber meets the road, all partners have to work together.

***

I remember my first negative interaction with a parent as head coach. With my first gig at the YMCA, we didn't have much lanespace to work with. Tuesday nights were the worst. I had every athlete on deck or in the pool at once. It was mayhem with eighty-five bodies being moved around a six-lane pool. The older kids started with dryland and crossed over with the younger athletes at six p.m.

As dryland finished one Tuesday night, an older swimmer made a rude comment to a younger athlete in passing. The younger boy was confused by the interaction and began to cry. My assistant coach overheard the brief exchange and stepped in to confront the older swimmer.

"You said something very inappropriate. I want you to say you're sorry to him. Then gather your things and leave."

The older swimmer quickly fired back aggressively: "You can shut up! You suck!"

There was silence and the entire team froze.

I quickly intervened and ushered the athlete out to the hallway. He collected his belongings and I called his mother for an impromptu meeting. The three of us sat in my office and the tension was so thick you could cut it with a knife. I don't remember the word-for-word quotes from his mother, but I did jot down a few notes.

- "My son reacted to something your coach did when she filled in for you a while back. She sat him out for no reason at dryland." My assistant coach had covered for me while I attended a Friday-night meet session. The athlete, who was normally well-behaved, had whipped a teammate in the head with a stretch cord. After multiple warnings, he'd been excused from practice.

- "We can take our money and business elsewhere. There are plenty of teams in the area."Genuine respect and loyalty has become a thing of the past. I couldn't believe she threatened to leave our team because we disciplined her son.

- "You don't want to mess with mama bear." Parents can take an adversarial stance when their children are out of line. The best coaches provide life lessons and teachable moments through discipline.

The conversation ended abruptly after she insulted my assistant coach and ignored all accountability for her son's actions. We made the decision to dismiss the family from our team.

Coaches are quick to blame children for their behavior. My assistant coach used to say, "Kids have changed, but parents need to accept the blame for it." Behavior is simply the reflection of the environment we live in. Kids can be disrespectful, inconsiderate, and mean, but seldom are these mannerisms intrinsically set from birth. Children are parented differently because family culture varies from household to household.

As a coach, I stay in my lane. I can't provide the teachable moments (behavior modification) a parent is responsible for. Parenting is difficult. I live with two children. Rowan and Eden are my life. They're amazing! They also misbehave. I won't let my love for them stand in the way of redirection and discipline. Misaligned parents pacify their children with praise and gifts instead of dealing with challenges. Parents avoid teachable moments by placing a tablet in front of their kids instead of talking through problems. Children need us. They need structure with amazing coaches and sports. They need parents for behavior modification and redirection. We need to embrace the teachable moments, constructive feedback, and discipline. Kids haven't changed. Parents have. Kids grow up in the environment and culture we've created. Amazing parents are mature, accountable, firm, and loving. Identify variance between home and team culture with each athlete.

Compromise is best when appropriate. I won't bend with policy, culture, and philosophy. I've been persuaded to change meet entries, train an athlete slightly differently, or provide free swim lessons to a struggling swimmer. I'm fine with these compromises. If compromise isn't an option and it creates a disruption, excuse the family from the team. A child won't work effectively with a coach if his or her parents won't support the infrastructure of the team.

There are *bad swim parents* and there are *bad swim coaches*. We form opinions of people based on how they stack up to our value system. Swim parents huddle in the bleachers, the lobby, a coffee shop and gossip about coaches.

"Well, this is how I'd coach the team. I'd start by..."

"Do they even teach technique in practice? I can't believe little Suzy does..."

"How do they come up with these relays? My son is faster than..."

If you care about their perception of you professionally, you respond to the noise. Managing a team takes guts and skill. And it takes a backbone. I forge on, knowing external critique is part of the job. I won't take the comments personally. Here are a few statements made about me over the years.

- I don't know how to taper swimmers.
- My practices aren't made for sprinters.
- I need to hire better assistants.
- I have to focus on technique.
- I need to praise my swimmers more.
- Dryland needs to be more challenging.

For new coaches, I have simple words of encouragement. The first is to develop tough skin and to not take the noise personally (even when it gets ugly). If the critique requires action after personal reflection, thank the parent for the feedback. We can all improve. Feedback is a gift.

Second, develop a culture that fleshes out bad families. Eventually, these families leave if other families ignore their toxic attitude or if they realize they're wrong and are too embarrassed to face the music.

Number three is the most important piece of advice: Be true to yourself. No one else knows the time and effort you put in. The majority of swim parents have no idea what my day is like. I'm on deck for five hours a day. We have an hour-long dryland. I'm in meetings for another two hours and create practices with another hour. Dietetics and management duties require another two hours. And I work six or seven days a week. Calling in sick or working from home isn't an option.

Meetings with parents are organized and structured. Set an agenda and email it to the family twenty-four hours before you meet. If a parent calls a meeting with you, request an agenda from them. Agendas set the stage for a transparent discussion without (or with very little) tension. Welcome the parents and greet them with a warm smile. Meetings are non-adversarial when you maintain positive body language and keep the conversation professional. Avoid embarrassing or antagonizing parents during the discussion. Anything you say may ruin the trust between you and the family. Remember, you can't put the toothpaste back in the tube.

Respect their thoughts and opinions, even if you disagree with them. Control the narrative when appropriate. Maintain control with objective (fact-based) dialogue and avoid suppositions. When the conversation is over, thank them for their time and feedback. Then, reconnect with them within twenty-four hours to see if they have additional questions.

If you need to take notes during the meeting, do it. However, don't let it detract from your attention.

***

Why isn't my son swimming faster? Why isn't my daughter beating the kids she beat last year? Why did my son have a bad meet? Why didn't my daughter taper well? The greatest coaches in the world get these questions. How many times have you read or heard a negative comment about a top-tier coach in your area? I can't believe people critique Eddie Reese and Bob Bowman, but they do.

Questions, concerns, and critique come with the territory. The big pink elephant in the room is a poor championship performance. Bad swims, bad coach. Good swims, good swimmer. Coaches are an easy target for poor performance. Athletes don't miss a taper. They miss a season. Swimmers won't improve unless they make the intrinsic commitment to be better. Parents seldom connect commitment, practice attendance, and practice performance with a championship performance. Since they don't attend practices to see their children train, they form a supposition. Children tell their parents a different story. "Mom, I worked hard today.""Dad, I went to dryland after practice.""Mom, I stayed in the entire practice.""Dad, I swam in a faster lane." When you challenge a parent's perspective, prepare for them to take it personally.

Coaches rarely *win*. Don't try to *win*. Several meetings end with a family leaving a team because a parent swears their child was a swimming angel. Obviously, you hold the objective data in your log book. Communication, weekly or monthly, is the key to maintaining a healthy relationship with swim parents. Championship swims are the truth serum for a swim season. Athletes don't improve in the end if they won't work hard in the beginning.

I had a swim parent who is a fourth-grade teacher schedule a meeting with me to discuss her 10-year-old son's performance at the Junior Olympic meet. Overall, he swam well, but managed only one best time out of six events. When we met, I provided her with the objective data. Per my log, he attended 60 percent of the offered practices. Out of those practices, he sat out or left half of them. It was a struggle to keep him in the water. I'd hear him say, "I like basketball. I don't like swimming." He wasn't having fun.

She asked, "How, as a coach, are you not taking responsibility for his performance and training? He should swim faster regardless of his effort."

I tried to provide an analogy. "You're a history teacher. Does everyone get an A if they attend 60 percent of classes and complete 60 percent of the coursework?"

She was terse with me. "Absolutely not. I provide the information, education, and support. But, no...not everyone puts in the time or effort to get an A."

I paused and then calmly responded. "Then why would you hold me to a higher standard than you hold yourself as a teacher? It's no different here. Effort and time on this craft yields the best results."

She understood and lightened up. They stayed in our program for another year before her son switched to basketball.

There are four "Buckets of Advancement" in my mind. I've shared these with a few families within our program. These buckets are effort, attention to detail, attitude, and coachability. Effort is the first bucket. I had a call with a family who told me I'm bad with sprinters. Ironically, they neglected the objective data. We were the smallest team in the city with four sprinters 21.5 or faster in the 50 freestyle. Their son, who was frequently called out by his teammates for not putting the work in, told his parents my practices weren't specific to sprinters. How many practices have they witnessed? How do they know what a good quality-to-quantity ratio is? Do they trust my experience and expertise? His practice effort was inconsistent and teammates noticed. Athletes advance based on effort.

Attention to detail is essential. We tell a swimmer to extend their underwater kicks off walls and starts. We recommend a bodyline change on backstroke. We tell Shirley to get in the water on time for warm-up. I had a parent rip me for asking her child to get in the water on time. If your child fails to show up at work on time as an adult, he or she will be looking for another job. Details are big things. I talked with a parent about their child's streamlines. She didn't lock her elbows and stack her hands. The parent asked, "How often do you work on them?" I paused and then replied, "We do almost 300 push-offs each day. Is that enough practice?" Make sure your athletes and their parents are attentive to detail.

Attitude is the obvious one. I can predict an individual's end-of-season performance based on a ten-minute goal meeting. On each goal sheet, I like to see one stretch goal (a tough goal that requires grit). I like to share this stretch goal with their parents. Stretch goals demand a certain type of attitude to get over the finish line.

The final bucket is the most important one. Is your child coachable and a problem

solver? Is a child willing to take advice and feedback from someone other than their parents? Swim parents love to hear about their children and specifically whether they're coachable. I've seen this statement on a T-shirt: "99% faith = 100% failure."

College coaches build great teams with coachable athletes. Competitive times are one thing. Physical attributes are another. Coachability provides stability within the framework of a strong coach-athlete relationship.

Develop a support program to teach appropriate modeling behaviors for swim parents. Though these classes seem novel and helpful, it never materializes the way we want. The *bad swim parents* never attend and the *good swim parents* show up because they fear they're bad. Make the program mandatory for all new and current swim families.

***

I've accepted athletes from other clubs to join my team. Transfers are a part of the sport. The choice to accept or deny a new family is about fit and culture. Will the family buy in to our culture? Are the parents, the swimmer, or both parties driving this move to another club team? What led to the decision? I check many boxes before accepting a family from another club. Unfortunately, the only box many teams check is, "Is this swimmer fast?"

I'm not a talent collector. And, I won't take credit for the athletes developed under the guidance of another coach. Senior-level transfers are appropriate if their current team lacks a firm culture, a plan for long-term performance, or little accountability. Harvest your talent. Be proud of your team. If your place among local and national competitors trumps your values as a person, you've jumped in the wrong boat. Loyalty is becoming a thing of the past with swim families and colleagues.

Why are your athletes leaving? Is it because of something your program lacks? Participate in self-reflection each and every day. Transfers should come to you. Athletes shouldn't be leaving your team. All of our transfers were willing participants. I have correspondence from transfers. I've had them put everything in writing, either by text or email, so their current coach sees the conversation from start to finish. If a swim parent engages another club coach in a discussion, there's nothing you can do about it. However, if a swimmer or parent from a team first encounters or engages an athlete from another team, you have a problem. Parents can broadcast their love for your team, but make sure they're doing it the ethical way. Educate your swim parents on this team policy.

The advice I bestow to young coaches in respect to swim parents is simple. Resist being reactionary. Don't respond to late-night emails after a long day. Don't react to the gossip in the stands. Avoid taking the criticism personally. Parents are emotionally bonded to everything their kids do.

Second, maintain a healthy boundary with team parents. I once watched a coach shimmy down the fire escape at the team hotel to evade swim parents. I have a colleague who's donned a wig and fake eyewear so team parents wouldn't recognize her when she was dining out (true story). Establish ground rules for communication. If ten p.m. is too late for a phone call or text, tell your parents. If a parent needs to talk to you, let them know when your office hours are. When you're off the clock, you're off the clock.

The third piece of advice I have is to be open to change and communication. Parents are a resource for you. It bears repeating: Communication is essential for optimal team culture.

Finally, understand your priority is with the entire team. We can't accommodate each and every request from a single family over the other athletes on the team.

"Sarah needs timed pace 50s after she warms up. Can you clear the lane during the twenty-minute meet warm-up for her to get a few in?"

"Can you run a warm-up in the dive well for Taylor when she comes in late to the meet? I know it may take you away from watching the swimmers in the competition pool, but she needs to sleep in."

Some requests are appropriate, while others can be disruptive. Compromise and be agile with swim parents when it makes sense.

***

I love my swim parents. I. LOVE.THEM. Hundreds of swim parents supported my family through our darkest hours. The most unimaginable horrors you can think of (the passing of our daughter, the unexpected death of a young coach, the passing of close friends, etc.) were absorbed by *every* swim parent and child on our team. The only reason I made it to the pool every day was because of their love and encouragement. The support didn't stop there. I was treated to dinner. A few parents cared for my finances. The team purchased gifts for our kids and offered to babysit after each meet. They cried with me. They hugged me. And, they welcomed me into their family. I wouldn't be the polished man, friend, father, and husband I am today without my beloved swim parents. I enjoyed serving you and your children and love you more than you will ever know.

Parents love their children more than they love themselves. When their child is rejected, bullied, or ignored, they feel the pain too. Before Sarah and I had our own kids, I couldn't relate. I do now. Each child has someone thinking of them, praying for them, and worrying about them every moment of each day. Treat each athlete with the same patience, compassion, love, and respect as you would treat your own child.

Chapter 20: I Walked Away from Full-time Coaching

Personal reflection and self-evaluation at the end of swim season helped me evolve as a coach and person. In 2014, I made it part of my daily routine. The exercise was simple. I'd sit in an empty room with a pad of paper and jot down everything I thought of for fifteen minutes. I wasn't thinking about snarky coworkers, my lunch plans, or an afternoon snack. My mind was clear and empty. Daydreaming became a routine. Whatever came to mind, I put it on paper.

Sentence fragments and shapes covered pages of notebook paper. Eventually, I scribbled outrageous ideas, audacious goals, and unreasonable thoughts. The fifteen-minute sessions provided me the opportunity to dream and therapeutically develop my plans for the future. Near the end of the 2015 long-course season, a common theme started taking shape on my notepad.

At age forty, I retired from full-time coaching to pursue other interests. The dream sessions forced me to reflect on my feelings. Work-life balance, professional challenges, a lack of family time, and unhealthy habits were part of each daydream. Coaching left me mentally and emotionally paralyzed. I felt "fried." My coaching lifestyle wasn't sustainable.

The exercise supported my desire to make a change. Additionally, it celebrated the attributes I value myself. I parsed a full week of dreams to record these attributes on a note card. Here they are.

- Creative
- Independent but a great teammate
- Responsible
- Risk taker
- Focused/goal-oriented
- Goal-driven
- Hunter mentality

- Motivated by culture and the mission
- Loving and helpful
- Empathetic
- Accountable
- Disciplined
- Problem solver
- Dreamer
- Leader

I followed these attributes by listing five professional goals for the next ten years.

1. Write a book to support swim coaches.

2. Develop a training program suitable for triathletes.

3. Invent a widget/gadget/product for youth swimming.

4. Create a website to mentor, support, and motivate our coaches, leaders, and teachers.

5. Partner with a friend to start a business.

The juice was worth the squeeze. Being a head swim coach was the most rewarding professional experience in my life. I remain connected to the sport as a part-time coach. Even though I'm not in the thick of it every day, I'm truly humbled by the friendships and relationships I've forged through swimming.

I hope the information I've shared helps you grow and shape a better coaching career. Until next time, have fun on deck, everybody!

Acknowledgments

I have many people to thank for their love, support, and enthusiasm with this project.

First, I'd like to thank God for putting it in my heart to write these words.

To my wife, Sarah: I love you! You've continued to support me through the highs and lows of life.

To my children—Corinne, Rowan, and Eden—Daddy loves you more than you will ever imagine and know.

To my parents, Henry and Carol, and my sister, Lauren: Thank you for never allowing me to quit on myself. I love you!

To my cousin Chris, Uncle Norm, Aunt Jan, Aunt Lisa, Uncle John, and cousin Leah: I appreciate your patience with me as I navigated through the ups and downs of life. I wish I'd spent more quality time with you, but you know how much I love you.

Thank you to Greg, Leah, Lucy, Landon, and Anne. I can always count on you for encouragement and support.

Thank you to everyone who had to deal with young Aaron. Orchard Hill Swim Club was my second home as a kid. Years later, Powel Crosley, Jr. YMCA and the Clippard Family YMCA became my refuge. I also spent countless hours at the Baroque Violin Shop screeching a fiberglass bow over the strings of my cello. I'm sure I'll miss someone on this list, but the amazing people who encouraged me include Mike Leonard, Sabrina Manning, Melissa Parker, Bob Aylesworth, Geri Sutyak, Doug Bruestle, and good ol' Mr. Campbell. If you were all standing in front of me, I'd give you a huge hug.

Monty Hopkins made me a better person through swimming at the University of Cincinnati. Thank you for putting up with me. I'm thankful for all of my teammates in college. I miss you all and wish we could share one more weekend at a swim meet together as goofy kids.

Though we've not stayed in touch, I have to thank Becky Smith, Dr. Bonnie Brehm, Lisa Andrews, and Dr. Kelli Williams. The four of you helped launch my dietetic career. I've matured if you can believe that.

Thank you to those who took a chance on me professionally. Those people are Brad Isham, Jennifer Mayer, Pam Farmer, Patty Tomley, Mark Perkins, Nancy Doak, Jim Brower, John Jacobs, Kevin Weldon, and Pam Butler.

Thank you to every assistant coach who shared my vision and listened to my jokes. You were my teachers, counselors, and best friends. I enjoyed the hard work we put in every day to make our swimmers better people.

My masters swim group was absolutely amazing! Over forty different people over the years came in at five thirty a.m. on Tuesdays and Thursdays ready to swim and put up with me. There are too many of you to name...too many...and I'm afraid I'd leave someone out. I love you!

I'd also like to thank the people who watched me grow from the smart-mouth I was years ago: the Wilburns, Fergusons, Crouches, Kinneys, Suggs, Kalbs, Alberts, Betsy Oriolo, Ragsdales, Hewitts, Hoalsts, Seithers, Kampschmidts, McNallys, Willisons, Simpsons, Helds, Borgemenkes, Mirizzis and Donnellons. I know I've left out someone important and I'm incredibly sorry!

Thank you to my Pivot Realty Group family. An amazing opportunity arose as I decided to pull away from coaching fulltime. Now, I get to continue my coaching in career development. The tremendous real estate agents at Pivot have helped me become a better person and man.

The amazing Jules Hucke edited this book (and didn't throw it in the trash when she read it) and Jonah McClure put finishing touches on this project. You two are the best!

None of this would be possible without the amazing athletes and swim parents I've worked with. I'd name a few and then, of course, I'd end up leaving some people out (and I don't want to do that). To the thousands of swim families I met through the years, I love you! You made this journey possible.

I dedicate this book to the loving memory of Corinne Rose, Brogan Dulle, Nancy Hecht, Marty Carr, and my grandparents. Always on my mind, always in my heart, and I've never let you go.

www.ingramcontent.com/pod-product-compliance
Lightning Source LLC
Chambersburg PA
CBHW080521030726
47592CB00012B/3432